He Loves Me

The Matchmakers' Guide to Dating Again
& Attracting the Man of Your Dreams

Nancy Gold Zimmer, PhD
Barbara Black Goldfarb, MHA

Published by River Grove Books
Austin, TX
www.rivergrovebooks.com

Distributed by River Grove Books

Design and composition by Greenleaf Book Group
Cover design by Greenleaf Book Group and Teresa Muniz
Cover images used under license from
©Unsplash/Lucas George Wendt

Publisher's Cataloging-in-Publication data is available.

Print ISBN: 978-1-63299-439-4

eBook ISBN: 978-1-63299-440-0

First Edition

Contents

Acknowledgments

Nancy

A research and writing project spanning 35 years involves a lot of people. I wish to thank the thousands of clients from my psychology practice and Elegant Introductions who shared their stories, struggles, and insights with us and trusted our assistance on their journey. It is in their spirit and substance that this book is possible. We use pseudonyms only to ensure their anonymity.

I wish to thank the greatest joy of my life, my son, Josh, for encouraging me to be the best I can be. I feel so blessed and appreciate you, your patience, advice, and support. You never complained about the long hours and helped me create this book from the first outline to its completion. You are an amazing young man who inspires me every day.

I am forever grateful to my family and friends: my beloved mama, Esther, who showed me the meaning of grace, unconditional love, and was my biggest and ever-present cheerleader; Al, my loving dad, who taught me about discipline and a strong work ethic; Ellen, my loving sister, expert advisor, and guiding light; Andy, my brother, and Shelly, who sustained me with love and devotion and showed me how truly remarkable a loving marriage can be; my two Cheires, truly amazing earth angels and my BFFs; Mindy, my loving friend and title expert. And a big thank you to the awesome team at Greenleaf Book Group.

Finally, thank you to my partner and coauthor, Barbara, my dearest friend, for your patience, collaboration, and motivating us to higher achievements. I am blessed to be on this journey with you of bringing more love into the world. Your spirit contributed mightily to creating the ideas, space, time, and energy essential to completing this project.

Barbara

So many times over the past years Nancy and I talked about writing a book based on the myriad client experiences we have encountered through our matchmaking practice. It was not until the pandemic that my exceedingly intelligent and tenacious partner and best friend Nancy decided that she would commit pen to paper (actually draft on the computer), and voilà, *He Loves Me* was created. Nancy elicited my ideas and feedback throughout the writing process, and so I am officially the second author of our masterpiece that will hopefully be a resource guide for women as they embark upon a new relationship.

I can't imagine traveling down this matchmaking road and chapter of life without you, Nancy, by my side. I have the utmost respect and admiration for your kind heart, generous spirit, intellect, and integrity.

To my family: I could never achieve any success in my life without the full support and unconditional love of immediate family who are my rock, starting with my wonderful husband, Rob, who graciously serves as general counsel of Elegant Introductions; my children Sammy, Ian, and Jess; and my brother, Scott. My guiding light and inspiration has always been my beloved mother, Selma Black, of blessed memory, whose brilliance, commitment, and zest for life lives within me and makes me always strive to be a better person.

Last but not least, we thank you, our readers, for trusting us to take you on a successful journey for finding the man of your dreams.

—**Nancy Gold Zimmer** and **Barbara Black Goldfarb**

Introduction

Are You Ready to Fall in Love Again?

In your wildest dreams, you never thought you'd be back in the dating scene again, single and looking for love. Yet here you are. And wow: has dating sure changed! No more sitting by the phone and waiting for him to call. (Now you're waiting for him to text.) No more being picked up at the front door by a suitor with flowers in his hand. (Now you're meeting someone at a mutually convenient destination for a first meeting to see if you want to go on a second date.)

If you're a widow, a divorcée, or a recently single woman who is ready for romance and love but aren't sure where to begin, this book is for you. Even if you haven't dated in years, we will start you in the shallow end of the dating pool and guide you toward swimming confidently toward the "happily ever after" you've been dreaming of.

We understand that this new dating scene can be a shock to the system for the born-again dater. It may make you nervous or frightened, or even hopeless. We understand! It's like you grew up learning to do the twist (or the bus stop, or the macarena), and now you're back at the dance hall, but they are doing a very different dance. We are here to calm your fears with support and guidance to get you on the road to hoping and believing that you can attract men again. We've helped thousands of women find their ideal matches, and we're here to help you, too.

Men can seem mysterious, but after listening to thousands of men who share with us repeatedly the same reasons they chose to go on a second date with our single ladies, the mystery was solved. We know what these men want, how they think, and why they think that way, and by the time you're finished reading this book, you'll get it too. (Hint: It comes from biology and goes all the way back to evolution and the animal kingdom!) We'll help you figure out where to meet great men and how to connect with them. We'll teach you how to identify which men are really looking for a relationship (as opposed to just flings). We'll show you how to avoid the common dating traps that will kill a relationship before it even starts. And we'll support you as you step outside your comfort zone and get ready for your next romantic adventure!

We get it.

We are Nancy Gold Zimmer and Barbara Black Goldfarb, best friends and professional matchmakers who believe that every woman deserves to be with her dream man. We started our matchmaking company, Elegant Introductions, to bring more love into the world. What we've learned is that a romantic adventure that is exciting and fulfilling is possible for everyone. Our clients find love because they are open and ready, and so can you.

Consider us your personal relationship gurus; your dating consultants, best girlfriends, your relationship coaches—and even your fairy godmothers. We want to show you the steps forward that will lead to developing confidence, attracting the right man, and cultivating a loving, happy relationship.

We call Barbara the "romantic Rolodex" because she has worked for decades advising CEOs, business leaders, professionals, and entrepreneurs. She understands powerful and successful men and their needs, their passions, and their demands. She knows what type of women they are attracted to. Barbara is our secret weapon on the dating battlefield—and she's ready to share her secrets with you.

We call Nancy the relationship expert because she is a renowned psychologist, matchmaker, and trusted advisor who has been supporting relationships for 35 years. She understands the human psyche, the science of attraction, and the dos and don'ts of dating. Her support and guidance, her insights, and her sense of humor will gently nudge you, all the while cheering you on.

Our trademark is supportive honesty and common sense. The result? An approach to dating that will change the way you see the world and give you greater ease as you go out to look for and attract Mr. Right!

Your Romantic Adventure Begins Here

He Loves Me is a guide to how the dating game works today. It's a collection of the matchmaking secrets we've learned over the last three decades—a combination of science, psychology, intuition, and self-awareness. We've boiled down years of scientific studies on attraction and dating to help you harness your strengths and provide the signposts you need to get back into the dating pool.

Modern dating is a journey of self-discovery. We believe that nurturing the love that is within helps you recognize the love that is out there. As you read this book, you'll get to know yourself better. You'll think about your goals, values, and needs. You'll challenge your limiting beliefs. With our guidance, you will review your romantic past and examine your unproductive patterns to prevent you from repeating them. You'll clarify your honest likes and dislikes—and the instances where your blind spots may need to be tweaked.

As you begin to use some of the actionable insights we've provided, you will start to feel more relaxed, confident, and inspired. You'll learn how to listen to your heart, listen to your head, and have faith in new beginnings. You will accumulate the tools necessary to attract the man of your dreams—the dreams of the person you are today. And you will learn to see that dating again can be fun! We want you to embrace the journey and adventure, and fully enjoy it.

That's why we've included Mike Valentine's cartoons: to capture those moments of unexpected humor that are part of the dating experience. We hope you will laugh at the absurdities you'll encounter as you make your way to the promised land of love.

Are you ready to embark on a new romantic adventure with a sense of confidence and humor? Join us. Take a deep breath. Curl up with your favorite tea, coffee, or cocktail. Let's start this new journey together as you head to a fascinating destination: your new life.

Chapter 1

The Ground Rules

In this chapter:

- How to get back into the dating pool—no matter how long it's been.
- Time-tested rules to keep you grounded as you begin your dating adventures.
- Soul mates and ghosts, and how to remind yourself that it's all part of the process.

Susan had been married for nearly 10 years, and she thought her marriage was solid. As her husband Paul's business started taking on new clients, he was behaving strangely. When they were socializing with his new associates and friends, he all but ignored her. He was climbing that ladder to the sky, and sometimes she felt left at the bottom, like she just didn't fit in. One night as they returned from dinner with a new potential client, her husband was strangely silent. As soon as they stepped inside the door, he turned to her, and as casually as if he were saying he didn't care for butter pecan ice cream anymore, he told Susan he no longer loved her!

After this shocking revelation wore off (which was weeks into months, not days) and the separation ensued, Paul was already busy dating and made zero attempts to reconcile. What a guy! At this point, Susan began to explore her feelings and thoughts about options for now and the future. She had just turned 40, and she was finally beginning to explore her own goals and needs. She called us for help. As we sifted through her goals, it became apparent to her and to us that she was ready for something new and beautiful in her life. She deserved it! It was time for her to date again.

Susan was stepping into the dating pool with a lot of hope, and a good deal of fear. Everyone—women and men—comes into the dating pool with their own stories and experiences. The more we've been through, the more wisdom we bring with us—and the more history. We encourage all of our born-again daters to be honest with themselves about where they've been and what they are looking for. With our coaching—the same advice you'll find in these pages—they go on to have the romantic adventures of their dreams.

When it comes time to get into the dating pool, everyone has their own approach. Some of our daters can't wait to get out there. Others are more hesitant. Some dive in; some wade in; and some just start by sticking in a big toe to determine the temperature. In our experience, only you know the right style for you.

APPROACH THE DATING POOL YOUR WAY

Whatever your style, by getting in the pool you are opening yourself up to experiences with new people. The best way to prepare yourself is with a healthy mindset. Before we let Susan get back in the pool, we gave her the ground rules. While these might seem basic, they're easy to forget!

Let's review:

- The first rule is that *you can only control what you can control* (and that's yourself). This includes having a positive attitude, flexibility, and openness toward who Mr. Right might turn out to be. Learn to be open to the unexpected—you may be surprised! Be willing to step outside your comfort zone.
- The second rule is that you have to *leave logic at the door*. Logic can be very rigid and does not allow for the nuance of personal differences. None of us will fit perfectly into someone else's idea of what "the one" is or should be. Logic can make you unreasonable and unrealistic. Logic needs to partner with listening to your intuition and your heart. Logical thinking relies on your past experiences. Remember this is all new, and with that comes opening and exploring the unknown.
- The third rule is *don't beat yourself up for an unsuccessful date*—they happen, and keeping yourself optimistic is the key. Just like the first rule, sometimes the date just doesn't click. You can't always control the outcome. With some minor tweaks, our coaching will help, so just be you!

Keep these ground rules in mind as you get back into the dating pool, and they'll help you relax and get the most out of it.

Not Every First Date Is with Your Soul Mate

Susan went on her first date in a decade with James, an elementary school teacher who was also divorced. She called us afterward to tell us how it went.

"He seems so perfect on paper," she said. "He wants kids. He's handsome. But he kissed me and I felt nothing. What's wrong with me?"

"Nothing!" we said. "It was just a first date. He may not be your soul mate."

"Maybe I'm not ready," she said.

We encouraged her to try again. She agreed to go out with Andrew, who also said that he wanted children and loved hiking and red wine, just like Susan.

When she called us after that date, she was elated. "I thought the date was incredible! I looked great. The conversation seemed to flow beautifully. We had so much in common and we knew a lot of the same people."

But a week went by and Andrew didn't text her. We followed up with him, and he said that he just didn't feel the chemistry.

Susan was stunned.

"I don't get it," she said.

The rejection hit Susan hard, and we worked with her to ease her renewed self-doubts. She felt she had completely misread his signals. As our coaching deepened, we helped her see how this brought back her rejection from Paul—and reminded her of our ground rules for dating.

To Susan, there seemed to be no rhyme or reason as to

why Andrew decided to not call again, because it seemed that he loved the evening and offered every bit of encouragement. Maybe he was intimidated by Susan's intelligence; perhaps she looked like the ex-girlfriend he wanted to forget; maybe he's afraid of closeness—or maybe he doesn't want to have children. Or maybe he just didn't feel it.

C'est la vie.

Next!

The Friendly Ghost

Lana is a client who placed an online profile because she was ready to find romance. She chatted with a man who seemed great via text, but when it came time to talk on the phone, he was gone. She had heard of "ghosting," and now it had happened to her.

We counseled her to be patient with the process and reminded her of our ground rules.

Even though someone has posted a profile for dating, he may not be readily available for dates. Is he shy? Insecure? Perhaps he may be nervous. He may be engaged with his routine, and adding a new date into the mix is a departure from that routine. Maybe work became busier. Maybe he was having second thoughts. Maybe he was just flirting, or looking for a fling. If so, he's not the one for you.

Lana chatted online with another man who wanted to get on the phone very quickly. Lana had a tight schedule, but she made it work—and she was so glad she did, because they had a very engaging phone call. But when it came to scheduling the first date, he was suddenly terribly busy. He ultimately did make a date with her, but then canceled it and tried to reschedule.

What was happening? She was confused, and wondered what she was doing wrong. Lana wasn't sure what to do. She was incredibly busy, juggling her career as a realtor with helping her oldest daughter care for a new baby. She was clear with herself that she needed a man who wanted to invest as much time and attention in the dating process as she did.

Our advice: We're all busy people. We have personal obligations, social involvements, and work commitments. If he won't make a date, move on. If he makes a date but cancels, give him one more chance. If he cancels the second date, close your heart and move on.

Lana allowed him to reschedule, and he was very prompt and attentive at their first date—and their second, and their third. They were married two years later.

In our experience, if a man is interested and determined to find his lady, he won't keep procrastinating about getting together. If he does, back to the ground rules.

Next!

Summary

- Remember to continually refer to the ground rules: these are time-tested basics every woman needs to know.
- Don't let yourself get hung up on early dating mishaps; they happen to everyone.
- The dating pool is an adventure! Be open to possibilities.

Chapter 2

Meeting a Great Guy

In this chapter:

- Where to meet men in person—and how to make face-to-face encounters go smoothly.
- Getting online? Tips for creating your profile and choosing the best photos.
- How to talk online: chatting, texting, and moving on to the phone call stage.

Lisa called us because her kids convinced her that it was time. She had lost her husband, John, in a skiing accident about five years before she met us. In one tragic moment, she had, in her mid-50s, become both mother and father to her teenage girls, in addition to becoming the family breadwinner. With the help of sympathetic relatives and friends, and a good therapist, Lisa managed to stay balanced while raising her daughters and getting them off to college. The tears still came at random times, but less frequently. Soon her daughters headed off to college. *It's time, Mom!* they told her. And they were right. Lisa had friends, two wonderful daughters, and a loyal goldendoodle—and she had room in her life for a wonderful man with whom to share it all.

When Lisa decided to get back in the dating pool, her daughters encouraged her to go online because that was how they were meeting their dates in college. They were so enthusiastic about their mom finding someone that she let them create an online profile for her. They started by selecting a few nice photos from Lisa's iPhone feed. Together they crafted the words that described her personality. At first, modest Lisa found it difficult talking about herself, but when she looked at the final product, she couldn't help but smile. She definitely didn't look like a widow with two adult daughters. In fact, she looked dazzlingly attractive and confident.

But when Lisa looked at her profile again a day after it was posted, she panicked. "This is crazy," she said to her daughters. "Let's take this thing down. Who would be interested in a near-60-year-old widow who hasn't had a date in over three decades?"

But within a few hours she received responses from a variety of men, ranging in age from the early 40s to late 60s.

"A 41-year-old guy is interested in me? What's his problem?" To Lisa, this didn't make sense. Even if he was kind of cute.

She realized that there was not only a new world opening up to her—but now she had a lot of questions to consider.

Who did she want to meet? What kind of experience was she looking for? What should she say to sound clever and witty? How much of herself should she reveal when messaging and texting? Is "Brilliant from Brookline" all that he claims to be, or does "Michael in Manhattan" sound more sincere? She decided she wanted to stay more local, so she made sure to change the range of her profile from 200 miles away to less than 40. And she realized that while she wanted to take advantage of the possibilities of online dating, she was also interested in getting to know members of her own community in person, so she became more involved with local social clubs and volunteering.

What's your dating style? Decide which type of dating pool person you are. Know yourself and what makes you feel comfortable. Then you can proceed at your own comfort level and determine the best approach for getting back in that dating pool successfully.

Where to Meet Men in Person

How will you meet the men who will fill your dating calendar? Well, if you want to meet your soul mate, you're going to have to date. And that begins with making contact with a great guy who is available and interested in getting to know you.

In the old days, people met through friends, through work, or through social organizations. Or, sometimes, through a mere chance meeting in their daily routine. In our current era, dating apps have taken over the way people meet, and romance has mostly gone online. Everyone—well, almost everyone—is logging on and evaluating dating prospects by swiping right or left on a picture. They're counting on a few words of personal description to tell them whether or not you are someone who they would want to chat with online, let alone meet in person.

How do you socialize? Are you constantly meeting new people, with a steady stream of possible dates on the horizon? Would you like to expand your social circles and meet new people you'd never encounter in your regular day-to-day life?

Friends and Matchmakers

Meeting through friends has many possibilities. From one-on-one blind dates to parties, or other planned social gatherings, this alternative has many advantages and disadvantages.

Your friends know both of you and your tastes, likes, dislikes, and backgrounds. This can help encourage a level of comfort and ease. Social media, such as Facebook with its "friends of friends," can also be a resource.

The drawback is that while looking to meet a potential partner, you may well wind up losing a friend. While it's nice to have someone recommended by a friend, it can lead to uncomfortable situations if you don't feel compatible with your date. When your friends ask you for feedback, it can get sticky. Several people have reported to us that they feel upset when feelings aren't reciprocated on the date when they've been set up by their friends. Either they didn't like the match, or the match didn't like them. The friend ends up in the middle, and you have to find a way to diplomatically bow out. And if the friend thinks the guy is a great catch, they may start wondering what's wrong with you. Are you too picky? Too difficult? If you tell the truth about their friend's imperfections or if he mentions yours, it can create an uncomfortable situation, to say the least!

Perhaps that's why, from the beginning of time, there have been people designated as the marriage authorities for singles. Initially, these matchmaking experts were focused more on pragmatic business mergers between families or religious rules instead of true romance. There is still a need for matchmakers, but happily, they focus now on compatibility.

Today there are approximately 1,600 matchmakers in the United States. Modern matchmakers have extensive digital resources to conduct their searches. Many take extreme precautions and do thorough research before setting up a potential date. They do customized screenings for you, and some even conduct background checks, examining personal records for criminal history.

Not all matchmakers have stellar reputations. It's very important to do your research and read their reviews to determine if they are reputable. Interview several matchmakers to find the right fit for you. There are many different levels of matchmakers to fit all budgets, and the cost is a factor that may limit your choices. Some matchmakers are geographic-specific or demographic-specific. There are varying degrees of specialized custom services.

Depending on their expertise, the matchmaker can also serve as your relationship coach and personal confidante. Choose the one that feels right for you.

Clubs, Bars, and Work

If you're into in-person engagements, consider a social club or another such organization, association, or meetup group as a place where you might meet a date organically. Social clubs are natural places to meet because that's why everyone is there! It might be a political fundraiser, a charity endeavor to feed the hungry, a tennis club, a bike-riding group, a place of worship, a political group, a travel group of singles, wine tastings . . . really, the list is endless! Check Meetup, local Facebook groups, and neighborhood websites in your area.

Be sure to participate in organizations that you really enjoy and are committed to. Choose something that you're genuinely interested in and you'll be more likely to meet someone who shares those interests—and often commonality leads to compatibility. Keep in mind that if you're dating people within a group setting and it's a group that you love and rely on, if you start dating someone and it doesn't work out, it can be uncomfortable to see them at future meetings—though don't let it discourage you from doing something you enjoy!

The bar scene can be very social and a way to meet new people, but it's a riskier choice. Yes, people flock to bars to meet people. They often drink to loosen up, and sometimes they overdo it. And yes, you can meet men at a bar. But when the alcohol flows, personal judgment becomes cloudy. We've all heard stories about people meeting potential mates in bars only to fall victim to bad behavior. If you do choose to go out, it can be fun; we advise a two-drink maximum. Choose a bar that you're familiar with and where you feel comfortable, and preferably go with a friend. If you meet someone you'd like to see again, don't give your last name or address or any identifying information at the first meeting. It's advisable that you take his number instead and send a text, if you desire.

Then there is the workplace. One in every four employees says they are open to romantic relationships with a coworker. Approximately 22% of all married couples in the United States met at work. It's little wonder that workplace romances are common: after all, you're surrounded by people with similar interests and common goals. You spend a great deal of your day with the people at work. If you're having a bad day, you might have someone to commiserate with. You may also have opportunities for extra time together, like lunch or carpooling. The key is to build a friendship first and see how things progress from there.

Workplace romances can get very messy. You may feel you're together too much, or you may end up competing for the same project. Ugly breakups can end up creating chaos in your workplace (or at the very least, make it uncomfortable for one or both of you).

While there is a great deal of opportunity, there are also company rules that clearly spell out what's appropriate behavior at work and what's not. You should know your corporate policy.

Romance between managers and subordinates is often prohibited. At its worst, these office romances can turn into sexual harassment lawsuits. Unfortunately, there's a double standard in workplace romances where women are assumed to engage in relationships to advance their careers, and men are assumed to want companionship. No, it's not fair. And all too often, it's not smart. Proceed cautiously.

Making Face-to-Face Encounters Count

You can hope to meet a great man. You can go online, join clubs, go out and socialize, and at some point, you'll encounter a man you might want to go on a date with.

What then? If you've been out of the dating pool for a while, it's easy to forget!

When you're face-to-face with someone you're interested in, you can use your words and your body language to communicate your openness to continue the conversation. Just take it slow and easy! It's natural to get giddy and nervous when first meeting.

As humans, we want to be liked right away. But playing it a little cool is always best. Be friendly, but don't overdo it. Don't act desperate or impatient, even if that's how you feel inside. You want to be somewhat restrained. From our work with very successful men, we know that their screening process begins immediately when they meet a woman. Even before the date, they're eager to see if you're easy or difficult. Will you let him take charge, or are you going to be oppositional every time decisions are to be made? (If so, he'll run away—whether he's an alpha male or not.)

If you want to maintain his interest, be flexible and easy-going. You might offer gentle compliments and sincere comments. Keep the conversation light. Let the humor flow naturally. Don't try to make jokes unless you're good at them. Don't use vulgar language or discuss sex, especially at the beginning. It sends the wrong message about what you're looking for. Discuss your personal interests or hobbies. Find common ground. Even more important than small talk is maintaining a smile. Eye contact says a great deal also. If the vibe is right, you might place a gentle hand on his arm when making a point—but don't do that within the first 10 minutes! You might lean into his space subtly, but not intrusively. The trick is to come across as easygoing and fun!

On Board for Online

Digital technology has transformed our society, including how people meet and develop relationships. Online dating is a platform created for ease, accessibility, comfort, specific searching, and convenience. With online dating, you're in charge. You set the pace. You can decide who to respond to, and if or when to respond. You decide if you want to meet someone in person, for a quick coffee, or for a meal. This is *your* decision.

Attitudes toward dating apps have grown more positive in recent years, with 55% considering online dating to be a good way to meet like-minded people. Recent statistics show that one in three singles is dating online. The average age is 33.8; most are employed, and there are slightly more men than women who look for dates online. Some are looking for fun, many are searching for a relationship, and yes, some are just looking for sex.

Studies show that more than a third of singles report meeting their partner online. Online dating is the hottest and most convenient means of meeting someone. It's an easy way to see if there are any sparks. It has numerous advantages: variety, ease, a huge population categorized by interest and age, and the opportunity to screen before meeting. Wow!

Keep in mind that there can be a lack of transparency or safety. Anyone can write anything they want in their profile—in fact, they may not have even written it (like Lisa, from the beginning of the chapter). There are generally no screenings or background checks, and everyone else you're chatting with also has countless options. There is a great deal of fraud online, including scams to procure money. It's a public forum where anyone can see your profile, so keep your information safe and secure. The only barrier between you and a bad choice is your own instinct. Pay attention to your gut feeling! If a guy sounds too good to be true, he probably is.

Tips for Getting Started

If you're just getting started online with dating apps, how do you feel? Excited? Exhilarated? Nervous? Unsure? All of these at once?

It's natural if you feel overwhelmed at first. There are more than 2,500 online dating sites in the United States alone, with thousands of new sites popping up every year.

If you're feeling tech-challenged, chances are you know a teen or young adult—yours or someone else's—who could set you up online and give you a tutorial.

Dating apps are very advanced and specific these days. There are apps for your specific demographic, age, gender, location, religion, sexual orientation, hobbies, and more. Whether you're a divorcée, widowed, or any other classification, know that you have a community out there just waiting for you. And you can find it with just a little bit of clever searching via Google.

Don't feel you need to make a snap decision—in fact, we encourage you to take your time. Explore various dating sites to determine what interests you the most. Read reviews to find out what other people are saying. Ask your friends for recommendations.

When you find a site that appeals to you, sign up for a month and give it a test drive to see how it goes. After the initial confusion wears off, most people report that it turns out to be fun, with lots of choices, options, and freedom to explore whatever suits your fancy.

Your Profile: Is It All About the Photo?

Yes, you'll want to create a descriptive and engaging profile that includes interests. Don't sweat it about being too clever; sincerity is more important. Focus on what makes you different from everyone else. (After all, everybody likes candlelit dinners and walks on the beach!) Telling him who you are and what you're looking for counts—*showing* him who you are counts more.

A good photo attracts. That's the reality. Everyone notices your main photo first. Men are particularly visual, and without an appealing photo, no one will ever get to your brilliant profile. In fact, some men don't bother to look at the profile at all and are surprised when a first date turns out to be very materialistic, religious, on the extreme right or left politically, or without any common interests—even though it was quite clear from their profile. If you decide to create your profile without a photo, don't be surprised if you get zero responses! Think about how you look at profiles: if you're brushing by or ignoring a man's photo to see what gems he has written, you're probably the first to do that. So yes: appearances matter.

Let's explain a bit more specifically what that means:

- You want to look your best in your profile photo—but also natural. That means just a hint of makeup, with no sunglasses and a simple but stylish hairdo.
- Make sure the photo looks like you. Remember the "truth in advertising" rule.
- Look lively and approachable.
- Make sure you're front and center! Men want to see your face and full-length body.
- For the secondary pictures, select images that tell the rest of your story.
- Select casual photos that show you having fun. Include children, friends, or pets if you like.
- Showcase your hobbies, your favorite places, travels—but mostly yourself. We've heard plenty of complaints about women who post photos of their trips around the world, and they're just a tiny speck, in sunglasses, in the background. Keep yourself in focus!
- Run your photo and description by a couple of brutally honest friends before posting it.

Breaking the Ice in the Digital World

Men are not generally great conversationalists. Be ready to respond to his initial contact online in an upbeat way. Make a basic friendly comment or ask a casual question. Feel free to start the conversation. It's okay to reach out first, but then let him take the lead.

Examples:

"Happy Sunday!" or "How are you enjoying your weekend?"

"Nice to meet you."

"You sound great! How's your day going?"

"I really liked your profile."

"Nice to find someone with a sense of humor / who enjoys cooking / who loves sporting events. Or someone so educated / who loves learning / who loves meditation / who loves working out or is such a good writer / who cares about the environment / who enjoys family and kids / who loves to travel."

"You seem fun, kind, honest, open, sincere."

"Tell me a little about yourself."

"Thanks for the like; you seem like an interesting guy. What piqued your interest in my profile?"

"What brings a man who's from Boston (or wherever) to these parts? Are you visiting?"

"What energizes you to get out of bed every morning?"

Note that none of these openers is complicated! They're specific—they let him know that you looked at his profile—and allow him to respond from there.

Picky Swiping: A Bad Recipe for Love

Don't let the multitude of choices in online dating keep you single. Digital dating can be tantalizing and overwhelming. There are millions of people out there just like you looking for true love—so be gracious, be humble, and be kind.

Don't get caught up in the trading-up cycle. These sites have a vested interest in keeping you aboard, even after you've found someone, and often keep sending you alluring photos to keep you thinking that you can do better. Unfortunately, some of these are fake profiles designed to keep you signed up (major dating sites have been sued for doing just that). When you find Mr. Right, work at it—don't trade him in for a potential Mr. Righter, a handsome, brilliant wordsmith who literally might not even exist!

Safety Tips for Online Chatting

Remember, safety is as essential online as it is in the "live" world. Keep these tips in mind:

- Don't give out your private information to a stranger just because he's charming.
- A legitimate date will not demand your last name, phone number, or address.
- Protect your personal information, including where you work or where your kids go to school.
- If you prefer, ask for his phone number rather than giving yours.

- Be suspicious if someone demands lots of info or asks for money. Move on.
- Be suspicious if a man is pushy or demanding. Move on.
- Be polite but firm when you decide not to meet someone.
- Frauds or aggressive men will show their bad intentions quickly. Trust your instincts here.
- A man who drags out the online chatting for weeks or months without making a date may not be relationship-ready.
- Someone who demands that you meet in person right away or that you send more revealing pictures of yourself is not looking for a relationship.

It's Just the Sound of Your Voice

Whether you've met online or in person, these days, people tend to text. While anyone can get onto the digital dating scene, when it comes to the mode of communication, we find that women over 40 prefer hearing the man's voice over a telephone. Brief texting is best just to confirm a date! Getting to know someone over text is not optimal. It's a challenge to get to know someone from an online encounter, especially one as abbreviated as a text message.

If he seems keen on just texting, let him know you prefer a

call. The truth is, you can learn a lot by the sound of someone's voice and how he expresses himself. If he resists, give it a little time and see how it goes. Compromise is the first sign of a promising relationship!

If he takes awhile to respond to your text, you should do the same. You should not feel the need to rush. If he disappears simply because you didn't text back within five minutes or a few hours, then you just saved yourself a headache. You also don't need to respond to his requests for calls immediately. Don't appear needy or anxious; you don't want him to feel you were just sitting around waiting for his text or call. Remember, you have a life too!

When you talk, the important thing is to be authentic and witty with your questions. You're trying to learn more about whether he's Mr. Right, but don't be obvious as you play Nancy Drew or Dora the Explorer. Your questions should be sincere and nonthreatening. If you feel uneasy, or that his answers are not making any sense, listen to your gut instincts and move on.

Keep the initial call short, maybe 10 to 15 minutes. Ask questions and then follow-up questions. Draw him out with open-ended questions (those that can't be answered with just a yes or a no) that get him laughing and sharing stories.

The basics to keep in mind:

- Be positive and upbeat.
- Be easy; let the conversation flow.
- Be interested in him, and let him know that you are.

This is not a sales call, so leave a little mystery! There is no need to rush the deal—but remember, the goal of online chatting and phone conversations is to decide whether you want to meet in person.

Most men tend to be extremely busy with their careers. We know you are too! That's why this book is about how to win the dating game and understand men. When it comes to dating, men are looking for a respite—an easy, positive, relaxing time. They will not open up to a woman who's annoying, difficult, or argumentative. They get enough of that at work! So when you're first getting to know a guy, remember to show him how fun, positive, and drama-free you are.

Summary

- Friends, matchmakers, social outings, or the office—if you want to meet men in person, remember there are many options!
- Be easygoing and fun when you encounter men; you'll enjoy yourself whatever the results, and so will they.
- Take your time to make an engaging profile and great photos when you create your online presence! You'll be glad you did.
- Don't forget your own personal safety, both online and in person.

Chapter 3

Warming Up, Diving In

In this chapter:

- How to cultivate respect and empathy—for your prospective date, and for yourself.
- How to fully enjoy your "backstage" preparations so that you're bringing your best self to the date—happy, confident, warm, and easygoing.
- Tips for preparation: an emotional, mental, and physical checklist so that you can relax and enjoy yourself!

Karen's story is a classic one. It resembles the challenges of many people on the dating scene. We use Karen's scenario as a life lesson for people who come to us for matchmaking, because her experience underscores how easy it is to make mistakes early in a relationship.

Karen was married to Bobby for 10 years and enjoyed a comfortable lifestyle. She was accustomed to dining in fine restaurants, booking upscale vacations, and luxury shopping. She never worried about what she bought or how much she spent. Bobby always seemed to have enough income for whatever she wanted. Unfortunately, Karen found out that she wasn't the only person Bobby was pampering. Her husband had a mistress. Bye-bye, Bobby!

Once she became a client, we began matching Karen. We set her up with handsome Dan, who was a true gentleman: honorable, kind, smart, professional. Dan was divorced, with a healthy relationship with his former wife and two kids in college.

On their first date, Karen questioned Dan about his lifestyle. Dan really liked her, so he decided to overlook this and go on a second date. He had financial obligations such as alimony and child support. It was clear that Karen was concerned about his financial circumstances and how it would affect her lifestyle should this develop into a serious relationship. To worsen matters, Karen pressured Dan to go to lavish restaurants on every date.

This pattern concerned us, and we explained to Karen that Dan was getting uncomfortable with her approach. But she couldn't see beyond his potential inability to provide for her lifestyle desires. Dan thought that Karen was cute, fun, sexy, and met a number of criteria on his wish list. In turn, Karen really liked Dan, had great chemistry with him, and felt enormous respect for him. But she was more concerned with her lifestyle than with romance. And that made Dan feel inadequate, insecure, and suspicious of her real intentions.

On Valentine's Day, Karen insisted that Dan take her to a fancy French restaurant. When Dan arrived to take her to dinner, she let him know that she was disappointed that he arrived with a box of chocolates instead of a piece of jewelry for her. Dan told her that he didn't appreciate the financial pressure she exerted. He told her that it was better they stop seeing each other.

Two years later, Dan's kids had graduated from college. Simultaneously, his alimony and child support ended. Soon he became seriously involved with another woman. Claudia, a physical therapist, valued Dan not for what material goodies he could offer her, but for his heart and values.

Karen regretted her materialistic attitude, but it was too late. When she called us, we listened to her regrets for a few minutes, and then we told Karen the truth she had previously ignored: that her materialistic attitude was a relationship killer. If she ever hoped to find a good guy, she had to be more respectful of the man and not view him as an object. And so our coaching began with Karen to open her mind and heart, to be a bit more introspective and empathetic, and to let go of her preconceived notions of what the "perfect" man had to be.

Backstage: Preparing for Your Date

So you've finally agreed to a first date with a man who is an excellent candidate for being a possible match. Now, it's time to prepare.

Begin by thinking about the best times you have had with a date—even if that was a long time ago.

We would surmise that your favorite companion wasn't angry, argumentative, or controlling. He probably wasn't flashy, superficial, confrontive, judgmental, or cold. He was instead the guy who smiled when you met, was warm and had a gentle laugh whenever you said something amusing. If this is what you like, then you need to create a first-date presentation that's going to attract this kind of guy. That doesn't mean be something that you're not. It means be aware of the way you're presenting yourself and how he might perceive you.

Preparation: Emotional, Mental, and Physical Checklist

First dates are supposed to be fun. This is not a job interview. Tell yourself: "There's no pressure here." It's easy to be a great date: bring your best, happiest, most attractive self to the table. After speaking with thousands of men, we have learned that this doesn't merely involve physical appearance. It's more about displaying *emotional warmth*. It's about caring and kindness, having a joyous demeanor. It's a *mental attitude*, an openness to be willing to share your thoughts, your ideas, and your experiences.

It's about expressing the beauty that's inside—not focusing on the beauty that's skin-deep. This kind of personality is the kind that makes a guy feel good. And it makes him want to ask for a second and third date. Of course, your *physical appearance* is also important. Men generally like a simple, attractive, clean look (think classic, not trendy).

Everyone is nervous before a first date. Confidence, a calm attitude, and a little primping go a long way to getting ready. The three ways to prepare effectively are to elevate your emotional state, enhance your mental attitude, and physically prepare. First-date rituals will become familiar, and they help you feel grounded and calmer.

Emotional

You only have one chance to make a first impression. So make sure you make the best impression you can! The ideal is to exude emotional warmth and a sense of ease. Here are five tips on how to attain this attractive vibe.

1. Exercise: Studies show that cardiovascular exercise reduces anxiety, improves mental sharpness, and has many health benefits. Seriously consider going for a jog on the day of your date. (If you don't jog, just take a 15- to 30-minute brisk walk.)

2. Meditate: Meditation creates a similar anxiety-reducing effect: a calm, centered, secure feeling. Meditation can be integrated into a yoga session.

3. Yoga: Combines both of the above. By opening the lungs, we open and let go from the heart. It combines exercise, meditation, and mindfulness. Yoga helps with increased awareness of the present moment.

4. Power poses (a tip by best-selling author and life coach Tony Robbins): Pay attention to your posture. Place your hands on your hips for two minutes and breathe deeply. Hop on the internet and watch the TED Talk by author Amy Cuddy on body language, or listen to Brené Brown on authenticity. Read anthropologist Helen Fisher's four personality types and their effects on attraction. (See the Appendix for resources.)

5. Be open: Being open-minded means that you're more likely to embrace the new—which just might lead to romance.

Mental

Prepare your mindset for meeting someone new. Guard against fitting him into a box from your past experiences by applying these eight tips:

1. Remember—it's just a date! Relax and release your anxiety. Replace it with joy, optimism, and positivity. Chill out.

2. Confidence—Not all of us have a lot of confidence. But there are ways to develop it. One suggestion is

to make several dates with several different men. This assures that you're not putting all your eggs in one basket. You will be calmer on a date, knowing you still have alternatives if this one doesn't work out.

3. Don't put too much pressure on yourself—put him in the "friend zone" for the night.

4. Don't get yourself stuck by prematurely thinking "He's the one!" This is life, not a Hollywood rom-com. If you find yourself doing this repeatedly, and these men keep "ghosting" you, it unfortunately may be because you're coming across to them as needy or even a bit desperate. Are you? No? Then check your infatuation at the door and realize it's just a date.

5. Open your heart and mind. Don't bring a negative mood to the table on the first date. It will drive a stake into the heart of your relationship before it even begins. Forget your preconceived notions about men and dating. Listen to the story you're telling yourself about this date. This is a new person, so let him show you who he is—in his own time. Don't *presume* who he is, whether good or bad, right off the bat. Broaden your definition of what you "need." He doesn't have to be just one way for you to like him. Does he?

6. Drop your baggage. You may have a bad taste in your mouth from a previous relationship. Remember this is a new person. Presume you're connecting with a man

who is a decent human being. Recognize your deepest needs rather than your superficial desires.

7. Prepare in advance some noncontroversial topics to discuss on the date. Keep it light and fun. What books have you read recently? Which films have you liked? Steer clear on the first date from discussing politics and religion. It may highlight your differences and what separates you rather than your similarities and what unites you. Prepare a few questions in advance. Not yes-or-no questions, but getting-to-know-him, open-ended questions.

8. Listen to music you like—nothing gets you in a good mood more than your favorite songs!

Physical

1. Remember, a clean and simple appearance—not an overdone one—is key to making that best first impression. Take a shower, freshen up, and lightly apply perfume. Being near water has a calming effect.

2. Hair: Make sure your hair is styled in a way that's most flattering. That look as if you just stepped out of the shower only works for twenty-somethings!

3. Outfits: Always overdress slightly above what he's expecting—but not as if you're attending a wedding or funeral. Don't drape yourself in designer clothes. Wear what makes you feel comfortable.

4. Don't look like you threw yourself together at the last minute.

5. If you're a high-powered professional, that's great. But take off your tailored suit. Clothes that make you appear to be in a boardroom meeting might depict you as buttoned-up tight, masculine, or a power person. So put down your briefcase, take off that suit, and put on a pretty dress. Men like femininity.

6. Makeup: Go toward natural rather than overdone. Try a pretty color of lipstick or mascara that accentuates your beauty.

7. Wear your smile!

Julie, another client of ours, finally put our advice into practice. She would usually put too much pressure on herself prior to the first date—despite being coached by us not to do so—repeatedly telling herself, "This is the one." Before going out on her first date with Tom, we asked Julie to try something different.

Early on the morning of the date, at our suggestion, she went to the gym and took a power walk. This allowed her to free her mind and repeat multiple times to herself, "This is only a date" and "I have other dates scheduled." She also took a long bath to relax, carefully selected a becoming outfit, and even brought out her hot rollers and makeup bag. All the time she kept humming to herself the Broadway show tune from *West Side Story*, "I Feel Pretty."

So, what happened? Julie felt much more relaxed, confident, and cheerful before her date with Tom. The conversation was engaging and fun, and now they are on their fifth date!

Summary

- Get yourself emotionally prepared for the date. Jog, exercise, walk, meditate, and do whatever it takes for you to chill out.
- Get yourself mentally prepared for the date. Don't pressure yourself into thinking that every first date will be "The One." Decide on topics to discuss beforehand, but be flexible.
- Get yourself physically prepared for the date. Physical appearance is important, which includes choice of clothing, makeup, hair, and overall grooming.
- Relax and enjoy yourself! If you're having fun, chances are he will be too.

Chapter 4

Setting Yourself Up for First-Date Success

In this chapter:

- How to make that first date a success—whatever the next steps may be!
- How to make sure you're accentuating the positive and eliminating the negative—and pitfalls to avoid.
- Tips for safely meeting new men in person and coping with the seesaw effect of new intimacy.

Peter, a divorced 65-year-old successful entrepreneur, had been disappointed with his recent dating experiences. He has steely gray hair that offsets his piercing blue eyes. His slim build comes from playing handball at the gym with fellow business associates. A well-educated man with a dry sense of humor, Peter was hoping to meet an attractive, engaging lady around his age, who would take an interest in his life, even though he couldn't really put his finger on what he was missing.

We have a great track record with successful men and know their challenges in finding a suitable mate. Their standards are high. After careful review of our clients, we introduced him to Debby. Debby is an independent woman who has a savvy sense when it comes to dealing with men like Peter.

As always, we check with our clients after their first dates. Peter did not sound happy when we called. He's not one to beat around the bush, and he let us know right away. He reported that she was very difficult—even more difficult than him. She asked the waiter to change their table twice, was argumentative about his conservative politics, and was fishing for his financial circumstances, asking about the kind of car he drives and if he rents or owns his home. As we counseled Debby later, this approach is very likely what pushed Peter away! With feedback, Debby understood, and her dating life greatly improved.

When we met our new client, Carol, we couldn't wait to introduce her to Peter. Being a lawyer, she is smart but not too pushy. From the moment they met, at a Polynesian bar, Peter was dazzled. Like so many of our bachelors' reports on feedback, he desires a woman who has a warm, feminine, gentle, happy personality. Delving deeper during our follow-up conversation, Peter told about how Carol gave him a welcome hug and disarmed him with her sweet smile. Over drinks, she asked him about his business just enough to be curious but not nosy. Peter likes talking about himself, so he really liked Carol's excitement about him. She was kind to the waiters. He was eager to have a second date even before the first one was over!

The First Date: Getting the Ball Rolling

When he asks you out, let him suggest the venue. Leave the ball in his court. If he defers, ask him to suggest his favorite place. If his suggested date or time is not convenient, respond with something joyous like, "I'd love to! Unfortunately I'm busy this week, but any day next week would be great!" Make sure to suggest an alternative, so he knows you're genuinely interested.

Starting at a coffee shop or some other informal meeting place is fine, and plan to keep the date to an hour at most. You want to take things slowly on a first date. A casual, getting-to-know-you meeting is always your best bet.

If he suggests dinner as the first date, go with his suggestion. Try to keep it a short dinner. Better to be initially cautious and take it slow than to be sorry. Be willing to meet him partway if he lives or works a great distance away. Don't be too picky about where he sets the destination; there will be plenty of time for the big decisions later.

You can tell a lot about who a person is and what they are looking for at the very start of the dating process. Remember that just like you, men are also looking for red flags! If you make a date with someone, don't change plans at the last minute unless it's urgent. This is a basic consideration. If you do have to change plans, explain why.

The right man will *want* to ask you out. If texting or talking on the phone has been going on for some time and you're ready to meet in person, but he still doesn't ask you out, you can make the first move. Simply ask if he'd like to meet in person. If he says, "Sure!" ask him what he'd like to do. If he's always too busy, it could be a warning sign. The only way to recognize the difference between "busy" (or shy) and "emotionally unavailable" is to pay attention. Your time is too valuable to waste on someone who isn't right for you.

Next!

Accentuating the Positive

The first step in every journey toward romance is to understand the fundamentals of male–female relationships. What really attracts a man to a woman, and vice versa, not just initially but for the long run? What hooks a man's interest besides a physical relationship? What essential qualities make him want to come back for more or run for the hills? And what's the underlying foundation of a lasting relationship? Every secret we share with you—from how to plan and prepare for a date to how to analyze it later—stems from these fundamental questions.

When Jim met Lisa, he was excited. He reported that she was gracious when he had to reschedule their date and accommodated his schedule. She met him halfway and encouraged him to reserve at *his* favorite restaurant. From the beginning, he felt accepted, heard, and respected. The second date went just as smoothly and now, a year later, they are engaged! What we have learned over the years is that men like happy, positive women who are nurturing, warm, and show appreciation for them. The men we have worked with are looking for attention and ease in their personal and romantic lives. What they aren't looking for are women who are critical, needy, or unavailable.

The goal of every single interaction men have with a romantic interest is to add positivity to their lives. Yes, that's what men want—don't you? Time and again, behavioral research studies show that people like others who make them feel good. This is particularly true with men, when they are looking for a romantic partner with whom to spend their lives.

So, when you're around potential love interests, you should:

- Be open about yourself, but avoid diving into your struggles, disappointments, and baggage. (Leave that all for the future!)
- Compliment when appropriate.
- Exhibit attraction physically, verbally, and nonverbally.
- Be light and flirtatious: physical contact, positive conversation.
- Put your most positive self forward in the little time you're together!
- Be present! Even if you have children, instruct them in advance that you're on a date and you will not be available for calls. Only answer calls in a clear emergency.

Eliminating the Negative

At the same time, you should try to avoid negativity. Specifically, you should avoid:

- *Being superficial or materialistic*: No one likes to feel like a means to an end. No matter how subtle, men sense when you're fishing for financial circumstances, and it makes them feel used. Best advice: don't ask any questions related to their wallet. Also, whatever your finances, keep that information to yourself. Where you eat and what you do should be less important than who you're with and his values, goals, or shared interests.
- *Mentioning your ex*: If asked, speak briefly and without anger. Say, "It didn't work out" or "We wanted different things." If he presses beyond that, we suggest something cute like saying with a smile, "Let's talk about that later. I'd rather hear about you." Going on and on about an ex is a red flag, on either side.

Remember—this is all about first, second, and third impressions. You might be the easiest, most fun-loving person in the world! But if someone only has an hour with you, they will assume that whatever they experience in that hour must be your personality 24/7. Of course you'll reveal yourself as more complex later on, as will he. But this needs time to develop in any relationship.

Don't be afraid to go by your instincts and gut feelings. When we worry about being criticized or judged, it's hard to let our guard down and just enjoy spontaneity and positivity.

Safety Tips for Meeting New Men in Person

There are times when your initial interactions before a date do give off warning signs—and you don't want to waste your time on those! Sign off online or on the phone nicely, but ASAP, if the guy exhibits the following behavior:

- If he only wants to meet at odd hours, or at a place suspiciously far from both of your homes—red flag!
- If he refuses to give you his number, even after you have set up a plan to meet—red flag!
- When you finally decide to meet him, select a public place. Before the date, share his photo and his contact info with two friends.

Anyone who exhibits anger, rudeness, seems drugged or drunk, or behaves in a demeaning or confrontational way should be left behind. Don't put yourself in jeopardy by trying to argue with a person like this; simply excuse yourself (and feel free to enlist a restaurant staff member or other nearby person for help if you need to).

How Not to Destroy the First Date: Romance Killers

Sandy and Robert had been communicating online and on the telephone for several weeks. The conversation flowed, and mutual interest has been developing. They decided to skip the cautious coffee date and meet for dinner for the first time.

Sandy is a 48-year-old interior designer. Her practice is thriving since she divorced a controlling, difficult man who often demanded much of her time, which jeopardized her work. But she's eager for male companionship again.

Robert is a 53-year-old doctor. He's adorably nerdy and very smart. He broke up with his wife five years ago; she was far too controlling and always placed him second behind her fancy friends. He's successful and works long hours. But he clears his schedule for Sandy on Thursday evening. They agree on a local casual Thai restaurant that has recently been reviewed favorably.

But then complications arise.

On Wednesday, Sandy's best friend offers her a free ticket to see *Hamilton*. She loved it so much the first time that she decides to accept. She calls Robert on Thursday morning and postpones the date. She does not explain. He's somewhat disappointed, but since Sandy is available on Saturday, he's encouraged. He asks his secretary to reschedule the dinner reservation.

On Friday, Sandy calls Robert again at work. He thinks it might be an emergency, so he interrupts a patient exam to take her call. Why is Sandy calling? She wants Robert to know that the Thai restaurant may not work for her; she's vegan, and the place doesn't have enough vegan options. Robert takes a breath and goes online, looks at the menu, and reassures her that the place allows substitutions. He now feels skeptical about Sandy, but minimizes his doubts.

On Saturday night, the date starts nicely. Sandy looks pretty, and she's smart and witty. He feels at ease. But when the menus come, she begins to complain about the lack of vegan options to the startled waiter. Robert reminds her of the place's substitutions, and she finally decides on a Pad Thai with tofu instead of chicken.

When the meals come, Sandy begins to ask the server and manager myriad questions about the ingredients and preparation. Robert is embarrassed. The two eat their meal with some uneasy small talk. Neither is happy. During dinner, Sandy takes three calls from her children. When the meal is over, Robert shakes Sandy's hand and leaves, without suggesting a second date. Sandy finds herself alone in the restaurant, wondering what went wrong.

What are the lessons to be learned from Sandy and Robert?

Robert wouldn't likely have been bothered if he knew Sandy had *Hamilton* tickets; he probably would have understood. But mysterious, last-minute cancellations are always a turnoff.

If you have any dietary issues, let your date know in advance, if it is essential. But look for solutions, not additional problems (work with a restaurant's options if you can). Don't make your diet the focus of your meal together.

Sandy once had a pushy husband, so she fears being controlled again. In this case she subconsciously overemphasized her independence—and it backfired.

Avoiding Dating Dead Ends

Avoid anything that will remove the flow of ease from the date. Specifically:

- *Criticizing and judging*: Remember that men like women who give off a vibe of ease. Men want women who are free, easygoing, happy, confident, and non-judgmental. They want someone to make them smile, feel safe, and who isn't argumentative.
- *Interrogating men*: This makes them feel like criminals or objects to be analyzed and dissected.
- *Who's the boss?* You have to decide something up front: Do you want a strong man? Or do you want to be the director of the relationship? You can't have two people in the driver's seat at the same time. Letting him lead is not about being powerless; it's about being receptive. If you want him to be a strong, take-charge guy, let him lead (or at least let him think he's taking the lead). Let him make the little decisions, and save your objections for the big ones.
- *Acting needy*: Despite what you might think, most men are not looking for a groupie to worship them (and if he is, he's not for you). They want to join two worlds together! Have your own life. Time and time again our male clients say they want someone passionate about their life and their work. The more you seek reassurances and validation, the less attractive you become.

Needy and weak are not at the top of a man's—or anyone's—checklist.

- *Being picky*: If you're a vegan and your date is insisting on a steakhouse, speak up. If he wants to get sushi in one place but you prefer another, see if it's something you can live with. Do you want to argue about who makes the best rice? Is it really that important to you? To put it in more specific terms: Would you rather be *right*, or would you rather be *happy*?

Post-Date Analysis

Let's say that you go on a date that gives you butterflies in your stomach. Lighthearted conversation flows easily, you both laugh heartily, and you have moments of silent excitement where you just want to fall into each other's arms. It might feel like a fairy tale.

After you go your separate ways, you can't wait to see him again. You go home feeling like you're in a dream.

If he immediately texts you, it might make you feel warm and fuzzy—knowing he was thinking about you and that he too felt that spark of romance. It might make you feel secure, safe, and self-confident.

On the other hand, if he doesn't immediately write to you, it might slowly eat away at you. If you wake up the next day to no message, the insecurity might start creeping in. Is he actually interested? Why didn't he write? Is he still in bed? Does he have a sleeping disorder? What on earth could he be doing until 1 p.m. the next day?

And finally, the paranoia: Is he dating someone else? Was I just dreaming? Was he just playing me?

Okay, easy there! It's important to understand that, believe it or not, men are people too. In dating and relationships, men have many of the same thought processes and reactions as women—and in this particular instance, they go through the exact same experience.

Let's go back to the ground rules and the fundamentals of attraction. You can't fix the past with analysis—you can only process, move on, and plan for your next dates. You can do your best to contribute to situations that accentuate the positive, eliminate the negative, and avoid dating dead ends and romance killers. You want to create romance, intrigue, and connection—and then you have to be patient and let the game play out!

The Seesaw Effect: The Dance of Intimacy

Now that we've covered the basics, it's time to teach you how to keep him coming back for seconds, and thirds, and more.

Note: This will *only* work once you have demonstrated a base of positivity, ease, warmth, and happiness.

The seesaw takes practice. During the initial stages of engagement, we suggest you lean into the opportunity to get closer, with more concentrated attention and thought. This involves embracing a bit of risk.

When apart, it's time to lean back and relax into your feelings. Relax and listen to your heart in the quiet of your alone time. Now you are in receptive mode: distant and more passive. Watch what he does and how he pursues you. Is he serious? Let him put his intentions out there so he takes the risks.

Studies have shown that men pursue women who lean back but are still within their grasp—women who show some interest but don't come across as desperate. Deep down in their brains, modern men are primal beings who still crave the chase.

This might seem contradictory given the concepts of positivity, attention, and ease, but it makes sense. Psychologically, when you experience something good, you want more of it—but when you can't have it, you crave it even more!

Thus, the key is to show *enough* interest—but not too much.

The secret is to make men feel great when you're speaking to them, texting, or being with them, while also being just a wee bit distant and a little less available when you're apart. It's a delicate balance because at the same time, you need to offer encouragement and interest. Be friendly, even eager—but not overeager. Neediness is never an attractive trait in anyone.

On the other hand, women who play *too* hard to get find out the hard way: for men, especially middle-aged and up, there are plenty of fish in the sea. They simply don't need the agitation, and they will move on without blinking an eye.

Life is unfair? Welcome to today's dating pool. But trust us, you can learn to swim in no time.

Summary

- Be easy to work with when arranging your first date—it's more likely this will lead to a second date, and possibly more.
- Be sure to accentuate the positive and avoid the negative: you want to avoid romance killers and relationship dead ends right off the bat.
- Don't forget to be attentive to red flags: your safety is important.
- Remember that there's a balance between maintaining his interest by leaning back, and playing too hard to get to the point where you lose him—so relax and enjoy the process!

Chapter 5

Dating Strategy: Your Guide to Understanding Men

In this chapter:

- How to understand being spirited as opposed to aggressive—putting gentleness to work for you to make men feel at ease.
- How to understand why men call back after a first date—and why they don't.
- Emotional attraction, and understanding men in the context of the animal kingdom.

Bob was a successful physician with a practice he had built from the ground up. He was nationally recognized in his field and was often asked to present papers at medical conferences. By age 52, he had numerous clients who always referred others to him. Belatedly, Bob realized that he had invested all his time in work—and none in romance.

Realizing that life was passing him by, Bob came to us as a client. He was an impressive man, both on paper and in person: six feet tall, with a solid body thanks to running. He had trimmed curly brown hair and an endearing grin. He shook hands with large but gentle paws, reflective of his skills as a doctor. He radiated kindness.

We asked Bob to recount his history on the dating scene. It was a short story. Somewhat shy, and never a barfly nor a social butterfly, Bob found it hard to approach women at the medical conferences he always attended. He also was a little cautious about mixing work with pleasure. Sure, thoughtful friends had set him up occasionally with a pretty lady, but the first dates at restaurants or at group picnics or classical concerts never went anywhere. By the time he came to us, Bob worried that he had focused too much on his medical practice and had forgotten how to address his own personal need for companionship.

We offered Bob a tutorial about dating. We started by drawing him out and getting him to verbalize his needs, his wants, his concerns, and his fears. We offered guidance to complement our matchmaking skills. Over the six months we partnered with Bob, we learned about his ideal woman: he favored high-powered, professional women, and had always been drawn to their intelligence and assertive natures. That combination stimulated and challenged him.

That all sounded great. But then why did sparks never develop? Bob explained the flip side of the situation to us. Very often, these high-powered professional women treated him like an adversary, not a potential companion. That is, they didn't leave their competitive nature at the office. On dates there would be powerful conversations, but time and again these women came across as judgmental, demanding, and difficult to please. Did it become a competition to them, we wondered? Were they threatened by his success? Or did they feel they needed to prove their own success to him?

We suggested to Bob that even though he *thought* he was easygoing, we could see that just beneath the surface, he was actually a classic strong alpha male. His career demanded that personality dynamic. He was nurturing—but decisive and assertive. And, as we expected, that personality accompanied him to the restaurant on his first dates. Even in the smallest ways, from choosing a table to ordering food, Bob's controlling, domineering side would emerge. The women Bob dated were responding defensively to this side of him.

Being Spirited—But Gentle

Bob was shocked—he had never seen the dating equation that way! Our assessment was this: Dr. Bob needed a spirited but gentle lady.

We evaluated our female clientele on many fronts and decided to match Bob with Sherry. Sherry was a successful corporate lawyer who was serious at work, but fun and witty outside of it. She was a patron of the arts and enjoyed baking at home. Bob was cautiously excited. We contacted Sherry and presented Bob to her, offering one special word of advice: on this date, she should leave her "corporate personality" at the door.

Sherry found our description of Bob intriguing. She was agreeable on all fronts, even allowing Bob to choose the little-known but popular Szechuan restaurant that he liked. She voiced no complaints, even though the dinner was a 45-minute drive from her condo.

The day of the date arrived. That afternoon, Sherry consulted with us for last-minute pointers. She felt optimistic and excited. Encouraged, she chose a flattering dress, set her hair, and put on makeup that would enhance—but not overpower—her soft, feminine qualities.

When she arrived at the restaurant, Sherry lingered a few minutes in the parking lot. She did a quick mental review of the tips we had given her. They included focusing on positive matters in conversation, listening more than talking, and dispensing with all expectations.

Both Bob and Sherry reported back to us later that evening. In addition to an immediate physical attraction, they had an easy give-and-take in their conversation. They kept matters light, discussing their respective careers rather than ex-lovers or financial issues—all good signs, as far as we could see!

What Makes Men Want to Call Back?

Why do men call women back? You might expect that it all comes down to physical attraction. Sure, that's part of the equation—but not as much as you'd think! The number-one reason relationship-ready men come back for seconds is *emotional* attractiveness.

What's that, you ask? And how do I get it?

Sherry understood immediately. Rather than interviewing and drilling down into Bob's work life and lifestyle, she engaged his heart. She parked her ego at the door. She wasn't competing with him; she was receptive and responsive. As we always say: you know everything about you, so find out about him!

Sherry's authenticity, interest, flexibility, appreciation, and kindness were well received. Bob was guided to be open with another successful corporate executive, even though other professional women he had tried to date were too often hard, critical, judgmental, and seemed to be digging for financial security. We knew he was relationship-ready. Bob wanted a serious relationship and hoped for marriage.

He called Sherry the next day. We had advised Sherry to leave a little mystery and play it cool. She returned Bob's call a few hours later. We had advised Sherry to make herself available to make plans with Bob, no matter how busy she was. Often women tell us that having a relationship is a priority—but then they don't make the space in their schedule for a date. You have to walk the walk, or you'll be walking alone!

Meanwhile, many men say they are ready and interested in a real relationship, but they are not willing to make the space or take the necessary risks. This could be a result of being hurt when taking a chance on love. Or, they have suffered a bitter divorce or lost someone very dear. We understand that a bad, painful experience can leave scars and fears. But if you embrace men with kindness and warmth, it will help them feel safe enough to move on from the past.

Sherry practiced our matchmaker secrets and put them into action. She opened up with full honesty about her career, explaining how it sprang from deeply personal reasons. She was warm, easygoing, accepting, inquisitive, and genuine, and as a result, she inspired his inner emotions. She allowed herself to express her feelings. That allowed Bob to see inside her heart and soul. She didn't display neediness or anger or fear, but instead offered positivity—and that made all the difference!

Emotional Attraction

Men often say they find that very beautiful women are more arrogant, demanding, and less accepting, perhaps because they are used to being flattered and catered to. To paraphrase Judge Judy: beauty fades; narcissism is forever. These men have their sights set on a more giving, accepting, nurturing, empathetic, kind, easygoing lady. Most seek a deeper, sustainable, meaningful connection.

Yes, we understand physical attraction is also necessary. But, as we've already noted, physical attraction alone is not enough. What endures are *emotional* connections. It's being attracted not just to the physical, but to someone's mind, heart, values, and dreams. These are the things that keep both partners invested for the long haul. This is the foundation that lasts not for weeks, but for years.

Understanding the Animal Kingdom: Alpha Males and Beta Females

In order to understand men, an understanding of the animal kingdom is essential. Let's delve into this a little more—because maybe you've forgotten the basics! Traditionally, men are hunters; they are alpha males. They do battle in boardrooms, making tough decisions with the competition nipping at their heels; they fight fires and police the streets and make laws; they do demanding physical work or administrative work and a wide variety of other things. At the end of the day, whether they have succeeded or not, they want a safe, warm place to land. While men like intelligent, accomplished women they can respect, they're also looking for warmth, acceptance, ease, and gentleness. While we're not asking you to change your essence, we're advising you to steer clear of projecting a corporate, controlling attitude on your dates.

Of course, things have changed drastically over the past few decades, with scores of women participating not only in the workplace but also in hypercompetitive positions and situations just like men. Many women have achieved executive status and take a back seat to no one when it comes to ambition and competitiveness.

But men have been conditioned to be competitive for centuries, and even those not naturally inclined to be that way will often take up the competitive mantle rather than be mocked or left behind. Hence men are used to being in control, and they are not looking to do battle with a woman who insists on leading. It's too hard to do battle at work—who needs it afterhours? So we urge you to let him make the little decisions, such as choosing the restaurant, deciding where to sit, and ordering the wine—everything to set the stage for a lovely date. You're the recipient, the one he hopes to please. Just lean back and let him do his best. You're not being a pushover; you're being smart and strategic!

Remember that this is an *emotional* interaction, not an intellectual or corporate pursuit. It's a restaurant, not a boardroom! You're here to see if you can move on from the formalities and nervousness of the first date to the relative ease and enjoyment of the second date, so that you both can get to know each other in a more casual way. Nothing kills the romance more than a competitive, edgy conversation of right and wrong, or a demonstration of power. Stimulating, not challenging, is the best way to relate.

This brings us back to that all-elusive quality men are searching for: femininity. What does that look like and feel like? It's the graciousness of being the receiver as opposed to being the giver. The man takes charge, as his ego propels him forward. Be appreciative. He calls, he asks you out. If you want a take-charge man, embrace your feminine, accepting, receptive side! Let him initiate, plan, direct, give, lead, institute, show you the way. Choose not to do anything proactive in the courtship phase because it's more difficult for a man to feel attracted to you if you push. Count on him to do everything. You just have to say yes and be appreciative.

Let the conversation flow, instead of turning it into a debate. Men prefer ease and warmth in conversations—not criticisms or evaluations. Don't come across as if you're trying to one-up him.

Here's something you might not know: in our experience of dealing with thousands of men, alpha men are actually quite insecure. Underneath all the bravado, they're just *waiting* for a woman to unlock their heart. They're looking for a partner, not an adversary. Your guaranteed path to dating success is through kindness, caring, warmth, acceptance, and approval.

Appreciation and complimenting him go a long way. Thank him for taking the time to get together. After all, he chose the restaurant, made the reservation, took you to dinner, and orchestrated this lovely evening, right? In other words, let him know that he's *made you happy*. That's really what he wants to hear the most. And remember: compliments flow more smoothly than criticizing and judging! It'll feel better for both of you.

A crucial part of your feminism is your natural inherent nurturance. It's a softness, a gentleness. While this may not be the way you operate in your everyday world, many believe this is a women's true nature. We have all learned to be tougher due to life's rigors and demands, but for success in the dating world, we're advising you to encourage the nurturing, feminine lady underneath. This is why many men say, "I'd really like to meet a teacher or a nurse"—because those are nurturing roles. Bring that to the surface! It's not about changing who you are, but rather about how you present yourself.

Life is a trade-off, and you have to decide what you really want in a man: a take-charge alpha male who often doesn't know any other way to be, or a beta male who lets you be in the driver's seat. (But remember: even those beta males want to feel appreciated.) There can be a balance of power, but that has to be negotiated in the future. Neither choice is wrong. The key is to figure out what you really want and go from there.

Summary

- Be light, fun, listen to his stories, and ask questions—let him know he is interesting, and show appreciation for all the preparations he did to organize your date together.
- Keep in mind that being gentle doesn't mean being a pushover. You can still be yourself; just don't compete with him.
- Showing your gentle side is what shows your emotional attractiveness—which is why men decide to call back.
- Don't forget to smile! It's the little things, but trust us: it will make both of you feel great.

Chapter 6

Matchmaker Secrets: A Winning Recipe

In this chapter:

- How to use our matchmaking secrets to be sure you're presenting your most authentic, interesting, and open-hearted self when meeting men on dates.
- Dos and don'ts for communicating—both verbal and nonverbal—that are more likely to lead to a second date.
- How to make sure your dating foundation is solid and your expectations realistic.

Life had been tough for Dave over the past year. Always methodical about details, as software engineers are, he couldn't quite get his footing back since his recent divorce. It was an upset to his structured, well-planned life.

Because his startup was taking off and consuming most of his waking life, he came to us for guidance and matchmaking. He was a serious, attractive man of 48, who was confused about what had happened at the end of his marriage. We helped him move forward and then prioritized his goals, values, hopes, and dreams.

His demands weren't unrealistic. He was clear on his priorities, which included a nurturing, joyous, smart partner of childbearing years. What wasn't on Dave's list: a size-2 beauty queen who was Ivy League educated and on and on (like so many of our male clients claim to desire).

So when Vicki, a 36-year-old nurse, walked in, soft spoken but friendly, simply dressed but very pretty, confident, and down to earth, with no pretenses, we felt we had met his match. Her prior marriage had lasted only one year. She realized, when the initial chemistry quickly ended, that it was the compatibility she had been missing.

She was now seriously looking for a hardworking man of character who was educated and ambitious. In her priorities, she never considered highly successful or a privileged lifestyle. All that she was looking for was a "good man" who would be a loyal, honorable husband and father, a man who could communicate and be kind.

Vicki was feeling good as she walked into the restaurant to meet Dave. She had prepared herself mentally, emotionally, and physically. As Dave got up to greet her, she walked over and gave him a gentle hug. "This is an incredible restaurant," Vicki said to Dave. "I've always wanted to come here. Thank you so much for choosing it." (She was putting into practice our advice of showing appreciation.)

So began the conversation on a first date between the two of them. Being a great planner, Dave felt good that he had selected a place that would make Vicki happy, and she set the stage for a lovely evening. The conversation progressed with ease, and they both found themselves smiling, laughing, and sharing interesting stories of their lives: where they'd grown up, their family histories, what they had studied in school, what they loved about life in San Francisco, and their favorite memory from college.

At one point, Dave started to speak about his marriage and then remembered our advice to not dwell but rather to say (without details, regrets, or emotional baggage) that it hadn't worked out and they had moved on. Politics and religion were touched on tangentially and didn't raise any red flags for either of them. At the end of the evening, Dave suggested they get together again. Vicki was overjoyed, and so the love story began.

Matchmaker Secrets

What happened between Vicki and Dave is the ideal scenario we want for all our clients. Let's review the elements for their success. Just as we guided Vicki through her reentry into the dating pool, we'd like to offer the same to you.

The key to success is making minor changes in your dating approach and attitude. It's all about your presentation. Establishing a dating foundation is simple. And we love sharing our matchmaking secrets with you!

We start with a few simple truths. First, men are as insecure about dating as you are. If you start the first meeting by erecting and hiding behind a wall instead of presenting yourself as a sweet, gentle, and kind lady . . . well, expect the meeting to be a short one. And there won't be a second date.

Stop Playing Hide-and-Seek

The goal is to improve your accessibility. So take a quick inventory about your attitude. Ask yourself these questions: Do you see yourself as an open door or a tightly guarded one? When you sit with someone, are your arms at your side or held tight at your chest? Do you lean back or look around the room instead of at your date? Have you developed a protective shell? Is your inner beauty hiding behind a wall? Do you look away when he's talking?

Be honest. We can all feel insecure. If you answered "yes" to any of these questions, then we want to look more closely at the messages you're sending.

After working with some of the most eligible CEOs and businessmen in the country, we want to tell you how they are perceiving you. Women often say, "Men are intimidated by me because I'm a smart, strong woman." Men really aren't intimidated by women, but they frequently explain to us that their frustration on dates is that they don't find you *approachable*. To them, you come across as hiding behind a wall.

Relationship-ready men want to meet women who are relationship-ready too. They crave a real connection. They seek a woman whose personality is like an open window. They want to be able to see inside, to connect through your warm smile, good eye contact, a friendly greeting. They want to be assured you are approachable and available.

Your Presentation: Make It Interesting!

Some ladies labor under a false and sad delusion: they feel if they show their inner warmth, a man will see their availability as neediness. So they close up and ruin their chances.

Remember, it's all in your presentation.

Ladies, face facts: we are all very hard on ourselves. There's that inner critic who sits on your shoulder issuing a constant stream of judgment. If you want success in dating, it's time to turn down the volume of the negativity. Better yet, change the station entirely! Remember: men are as afraid and insecure as you are, so exhibit an open, welcoming impression. It's time to hit the reset button and give yourself a personality reboot.

Immediate Gratification on the Dating Scene

Our best advice from decades of working with the world's most successful men: *They want to get to know you as quickly as possible. Yes, that's the secret to success on the dating scene.*

We want you to create attraction—and it's not just physical.

Men are interested in seeing your emotional, heartfelt, comfortable selves; that quality is just as important as physical beauty.

Look at it from his perspective. Your successful man has just been through a very hardcore workday. He's emotionally exhausted. The last thing he wants is to guess how you're feeling. He prefers that you're an open book emotionally. He prefers to meet an honest, soulful lady. Be certain not to frustrate or bore him by being mysterious. Excite him: inquire into his motivations, passions, family, dreams, goals, philosophy, commitments. We have the secret. Ask meaningful, heart-centered questions. When you do this, your man will feel more connected. Connected men are more attracted.

The Real Deal: Be Authentic

Be authentic—that is how you connect to a man. This does not mean you should tell him your life story or spill all of your heartaches. Of course you can talk about your life, but omit the heartaches on the first few meetings. Be sure to keep it positive, easy, and light. It's not time to be a totally open book yet. Let him see the best parts of you—who you are in your heart and in your soul. Opening your heart is different than being completely vulnerable. We don't advise that on your first few dates. There's a difference between opening your heart for a real connection and opening your heart and falling in love out of need.

A man feels his true value when he can do things for you—when he makes you happy and when you allow him to adore you. Let him see and experience the adorable you. Let him experience your confidence and softness, assuring emotional connection and safety.

Lean In, Then Lean Back

We have already touched on the process of leaning in and then leaning back. Let's go a little deeper into this concept.

When you're on a date, it's the time to be open, honest, and real. Give him a taste of something great (that's leaning in). At the same time, it's important to maintain a little mystery: for example, when you're not with him, don't be immediately available when he calls or texts. That's when you withdraw a bit and lean back.

It's a delicate balance, but it's important to show interest *and* keep a little distance. This also protects you. Here's where you let him pursue you. This is the mating dance (the dance of intimacy we've mentioned before). Keep it up until you two have forged a committed relationship. Then you can relax a bit and be more accessible.

The first date is a test. You're being observed and evaluated as a potential mate, based on your presentation. Since we're all multifaceted, why not show up with your most favorable side? Tell him about your good deeds; be sincere. Men look for clues into who you are. Extend your easy side throughout the night—in every aspect, from the way you communicate with this new man to the way you order your meal and treat the waiters.

IT'S STILL THE ANIMAL KINGDOM... LET MEN DO THE ASKING

And keep that sunny disposition in the dinner conversation. Ask questions about him and his interests, dreams, desires, and joys. Don't ask questions that probe too deeply, and don't ask about his ex or his finances. Avoid putting him on the defensive. If you seem too difficult, superficial, or dramatic, that will be a red flag for him.

Dos and Don'ts

So how do we avoid raising those red flags so that he likes you enough to ask you out again? Easy! Here's our handy checklist:

Dos

- Be authentic.
- Just go with the flow—don't complain about table selection, loudness, or sitting near the window or air conditioning, and so on.
- Remember: men want *ease* in a partner. They have enough stress in the rest of their lives. Be joyous.
- Compliment his choice of restaurant.
- Ask about his hobbies: what he likes to do in his spare time.
- Listen more and speak less. You know everything about you; find out about him.
- Don't answer your phone unless it's an emergency.
- Be polite to the waiters.
- Use good body language, smile, lean in, maintain eye contact, face him.

Don'ts

- Talking about the wedding you want, or how many kids.
- Discussing former relationships or bad dating experiences.

- Dwelling on personal difficulties and struggles—keep it upbeat.
- Asking about a second date—wait until he mentions it.

Solid as a Rock: Your Dating Foundation

It's important to clarify your own dating foundation before launching yourself back out into the dating world. Here, we lay out for you our three-part method of self-evaluation so that you know who you are and how you're being perceived.

First

The foundation we want you to bring to your date is self-confidence and self-respect. Don't act like you desperately need a man to define and complete you.

Self-confidence and self-respect:

- Influence your life choices
- Give you a positive attitude and outlook
- Help you maximize your potential
- Contribute to positive mental health
- Open you up to change and new challenges

With a solid foundation of self-confidence and self-respect, you'll love and accept yourself and be your fullest and best self without fear.

Second

How do you communicate? What are you communicating? It's important to explore how to present yourself and learn how to respond both nonverbally and verbally.

Ask yourself: What am I communicating to my date through my words? How would I feel if I were sitting in his place? Does he find me easy to talk with? What do I need to change?

Verbal communication is anything that comes out of your mouth: attitude, tone, pitch, the speed of your words, emotion, intonation, casual vs. formal speech, clarity of speech, voice modulations, and volume.

Words should be softly spoken. Talk slowly, laugh frequently, modulate your volume (let him lean in a little to hear you), and use an upbeat pitch to convey a happy tone.

Verbal Communication

- Attitude, tone, pitch
- Speed of words, emotion, intonation
- Casual speech, formal speech, clarity of speech
- Voice modulations, volume

Nonverbal communication is just as essential as what you are saying. All of the things below contribute to how you're perceived.

Nonverbal Communication

- Facial expressions, smiles
- Language, body movements
- Gestures
- Facial expression
- Posture
- Eye contact
- Touch
- Overall body language
- Body movements

Effective nonverbal communication includes smiling, looking him in the eye warmly, leaning forward and sitting up straight, and holding your body in a relaxed and open manner, arms at your side. Walk lightly. Give him a gentle hug at the beginning and end of the evening, and touch his hand once or twice during the evening, if you're comfortable.

The combination of verbal and nonverbal communication shows your gentleman your attitude toward him, how approachable you are, how open you are, how you express yourself, and what your mood is, as communicated through the emotion in your voice.

Third

How does a man benefit, at a deep level, from being with you? Ask yourself:

- How are they reading you: your intentions, self-esteem, availability, and emotional stability?
- Will you be easy to be with? Will you be kind, or do you seem judgmental?
- Will you smooth his ruffled feathers at the end of a hard day?
- Will you be his best friend and make his life easier?
- Will you be like a comfortable pair of shoes at the end of the day? Will you be supportive and unconditional?

Be aware of how you're coming across. Then make necessary minor adjustments. Once you do that, you will better know yourself and feel more self-assured. That's when it will be time to embrace self-confidence and stop second-guessing yourself.

Your Wish List: Realistic vs. Unrealistic Expectations

A very serious question we always ask clients is this: Who are you looking for—and who's looking for you?

It's time to assess if you have some unrealistic expectations in your search for love. This entails honestly looking at these preconceived notions and realizing how unhelpful these expectations can be. Such behavior squashes dreams and leads to disappointment and failure.

But you can sidestep self-sabotaging expectations. Dump the erroneous thinking, even though it's hard to relinquish. (We get it!) Instead, allow new beliefs to grow and ideas to flourish. You will find it's much better to be looking at your dreams more realistically, with a new lens.

When our clients are back on the dating scene after a long-term relationship, we ask them to share their wish list. We find they often come in with the same lists they had 10, 20, and 30 years ago. These are outdated lists with unrealistic expectations, which inevitably lead to disappointment.

Expecting Sparks: Dating Chemistry

Many look for sexual sizzle with a new partner—the physical attraction that we call chemistry.

That's always a great thing. But it's not the only thing! There has to be more compatibility between the two of you if you want a relationship to last.

We know you can't start a fire without a spark, but unfortunately that spark often burns out. We have seen many people go for the chemistry alone and disregard incompatible traits. And when the sexual buzz fades—and it's bound to fade—they are left feeling unsatisfied in their relationship. The result? The relationship breaks down and they start distancing, looking or hoping for something different.

Science explains that the chemistry phenomenon lasts only about two years before the magic begins to fade. What's left? Hopefully something substantial, such as shared values, interests, political views, hobbies, or family ties. Sexual heat may cool, but a substantial foundation that's been cultivated over the years will endure.

This is why one of our essential matchmaker secrets includes diving deeper. Try not to simply consider the sexual tingle; look deeper for the connection that inspires.

Consider five dating goals, in order:

- Bring your authentic self to the table and connect beyond the superficial.
- Get him to ask you out again—that way you have the option of deciding whether you want to or not.
- Allow yourself to be open. Think about how you *feel* when you're with him. How does the energy between the two of you seem?
- Overlook any small missteps he might have made when you first meet. He's only human, and we all make mistakes. Reserve your judgment—you may be missing out on a great guy!
- Don't set your standards too high. Give him a chance; he doesn't know your personal rule book and what's expected of him.

Summary

- Be authentic! Remember, men want to get to know you right away.
- Don't forget to lean in (and then lean out a little). Perfecting that dance of intimacy is what will get him to call you again.
- Think about the dos and don'ts for communicating—are you aware of how you're coming across?
- Is your dating foundation a solid one, or do you have work to do to present self-confidence and self-respect? Have you assessed whether your expectations are realistic or unrealistic?
- Remember that physical chemistry is only the beginning! Give him a chance, so that you get to know the important things.

Chapter 7

It's Up to You: Another Date?

In this chapter:

- How to analyze the first date to determine whether you want to go on a second.
- Examining your wants and needs—and learning the crucial difference between them for lasting happiness.
- How to broaden your lens, discard preconceived notions and patterns, and avoid falling into the trap of seeking Mr. Perfect.

Searching for Mr. Perfect had not served our client Cindy very well. Cindy, 65, was an attractive, well-read woman—but she had been single for 10 years. She felt out of her depth when reentering the dating world. Cindy went on every date we found for her, but she seemed to find something not quite right with each match we introduced to her. She would call us after every date and sum up the evening every time by using the same words: "I don't know, I just didn't feel any chemistry."

This frustrating pattern had gone on for months. One day Cindy came to us and asked, "What can I do differently?"

This was a breakthrough. Cindy was now ready for real change. So we began coaching her, confirming that her judgments and criticisms were a defense mechanism, an automatic response rising from Cindy's fear of getting close—and getting hurt again.

Our advice: "How about trying a new approach? After your next match, make a list of everything he did right, not wrong."

Cindy promised to give it a test run. She went on a first date with Jay, an optometrist. Jay was a well-dressed, nice-looking man. But he wasn't the knight in shining armor that Cindy was usually looking for. Jay was not gorgeous, not tall and well-built. He also had one young daughter for whom he was paying child support.

Up until this time, Cindy would have considered many aspects of Jay's profile as nonstarters: looks, height, a child from a previous marriage, and financial obligations. But Cindy worked hard to squelch her judgmental side. Their date at an Italian restaurant was fun. And Jay was warm and chatty, and not the nerd she had been worried about.

Taking our advice, Cindy went home and wrote down a list of characteristics about Jay that pleased her. She called us the next day and read a list of 15 items, from his stylish glasses to his old-fashioned polite manners, to the dimples that showed when he smiled. In addition, she found there was common ground in life goals, values, love of family, religion, and politics. After reading the list to us, Cindy realized, to her own surprise, that she found Jay to be a lovely candidate for a second date.

Cindy and Jay have been dating now for several months and are getting ready to take their first vacation to Martinique together. Lesson: accentuate the positive!

After the First Date

The goal is to understand the first-date results—and there is much to be learned here. We always advise clients: if he calls to go out again, then take him up on his offer. You might discover a different person the second time around.

Why? So many of our dates seem to not click on the first date. Consider all the jitters. The pressure. The nerves.

Many clients report a 180-degree turn after the second or even third date. How can that be? Well, on a second date, it's more likely that both parties are calmer, which means they're more likely to enjoy themselves. They drop the masks (but not during the pandemic!) and defensive behavior.

If he doesn't call, don't take it personally. After all, he doesn't even know the *real* you. He just got a taste of your personality and only met your first-date "representative." Look forward to the next man and the next date, and keep optimism afloat.

If your date calls after a bit of time—even if it's weeks afterward—don't respond with a negative vibe. He may be cautious, busy, involved with business.

The bottom line is that you really don't know *him*, either. Still, it's always better to respond with grace rather than anger. After all, what will you gain by responding with anger or sarcasm? Those are tactics that will definitely make you lose him.

If he never calls, that's a different story. You can stew or you can think about what happened. But don't call him—his message is clear.

Maybe a little self-reflection is not bad at this point. We suggest that you review the evening in your mind. Perhaps you'll identify some moments where you were not your best. Moments when you were not receptive, or perhaps you were sarcastic. Try to remember the story you were telling yourself in your mind during the date. Was it positive? Was it fear-based, angry, or disappointing? These are areas for you to look at and perhaps change. Learn from the past to strengthen your dating future.

That being said, it may not be anything you did at all. Maybe you look like an unpleasant ex he had. Maybe he's seeing someone else or just looking for a fling. Or maybe he's just a jerk. Whatever the case, self-reflection doesn't mean beating yourself up. It's a learning experience. The most common answer is simple: you simply didn't mesh. And that's okay.

You will save yourself a lot of gray hairs if you don't blame yourself for every date that goes nowhere. Not every meeting will result in your shiny engagement ring. Extreme self-examination and obsessional self-scolding will not help your self-esteem. If you think every bad date was your fault, then you'll fall into the trap of not liking yourself and trying too hard to fix something that doesn't need to be fixed.

Let's return to this nonjudgmental stance: a little self-examination is always good before you go out on that next date.

Ask yourself the following questions:

- How did you feel going into the date?
- Did you talk too much?
- Did you listen enough?
- Did you complain, or were you positive?
- Did you discuss your struggles, hardships, kids, exes, or difficulties?
- Was he responsive to your stories?
- Were you attentive to his stories?
- What was his body language like, and what were your nonverbals like?
- Did you smile a lot and maintain eye contact?
- Did you give off a vibe of warmth, approachability, kindness, confidence?
- Were you arrogant?

- Did you try to lead?
- Could you see yourself on a second date with him?
- Did you ask emotional questions, such as: "What do you love about this city? / What's your favorite part of your job? / What was dinner like at your table growing up?/ What's your favorite trip? / What's on your bucket list?"
- Did you stay away from politics?

Do You Want a Second Date?

Was the first date only so-so? Before you write him off, explore the following:

- Look at your essential *needs*. Prioritize the top four aspects of a man that are most important to you.
- Write them down for extra self-understanding.
- Now go down the checklist. Does he meet your four top needs?
- What were the worst things he did on the date (splitting the check, being late, etc.)? Was this the result of a bad habit, or of bad character?
- Are your standards and expectations reasonable?

Do you really want to write him off? What does your list reveal? What does your gut say? Remember that we said a first date can be crazy. It may not show either of you at your best, so it may be wise to give him—and yourself—another chance.

Forgive him for any missteps—and forgive yours as well.

Reconsider your unbreakable rules and expectations. Maybe some of these need breaking!

Remember that life is short: separate your fantasies (what you want) from your essentials (what you need).

Don't overgeneralize one behavior that showed up that night. Do you want to be judged by your worst moment on the date? Should you be? Neither should he. Don't assume this behavior is a personality trait, or a character flaw.

His goal is to make you like him. He needs positive feedback or he may lose confidence. Remember that men are insecure too.

Our goal here is to help you open the aperture. Accept him on his terms—and then explore him further. You might find some pleasant surprises!

Needs vs. Wants

Many of us have wish lists that we hold on to when looking for our future partners.

These lists are helpful in clarifying and refining our wants and needs. Often, great relationships require us to change our carefully planned recipes for happily ever after. To paraphrase the Rolling Stones, you can't always get what you want, but if you try, you might find that you get what you need. Understanding the differences between our needs and our wants can save us a world of heartache and disappointment. It may be necessary to look past your superficial desires in order to find someone who would be a great life partner for you.

True needs are core values. For example: religion or spiritual faith; wanting children; family involvement; honesty; communication styles; goals; character. Things like height, hair color, type of car, or liking football are not core values. We have found that people often gloss over what their essential needs are—and go with their desires instead. When goals and values are divergent in a couple, this doesn't bode well for a happy relationship.

It's vitally important to be deliberate about whom you date and enter into a relationship with. Although people think similarities are most important, that doesn't hold up when we view the research of happy, successful couples.

So, you ask, am I guessing when I say, "He's not for me?"

Most of us don't really know what we *need*. We may know what we *want*—but needs and wants are very different.

We have seen some of our clients have standards and a wish list that may be too specific, too long, and often too superficial. If you think this is you, please read on. One of our happily-ever-after introductions involved a man three inches shorter than the woman. Maybe other people think that's strange. They couldn't care less. Good for them!

We want to help you look through and evaluate your laundry list of must-haves (needs) and what you only *think* are must-haves. Do you worry too much about what other people think? Once you look closer, you may find you see things differently.

Maybe you find that you can actually be happy with someone who has most of what you're looking for. Perhaps he doesn't have to be six feet tall, or uber-successful, or an Ivy League graduate. Is it possible for you to accept a wonderful long-term partner who doesn't check all the boxes?

Think of it this way: over our 30 years of helping people navigate the dating world, no one ever looked back after a loving long-term relationship and said, if only he were two inches taller.

Compatibility vs. Chemistry

Once we distinguish between our needs and wants, we can move forward.

Of course, many people say the key to a successful relationship is chemistry. They are talking about sex appeal, of course. And yes, sexual attraction is a nice thing at the start of a relationship.

We have found that when many people start to date, their needs go out the window when chemistry enters. But that's not everything you need. The essential feature for a long-term sustainable relationship is compatibility and connection.

What does that mean?

It's the ability to weather the ups and downs of life together, to be on the same page with understanding, empathy, and a deep love. Of course, you must have some attraction to your potential partner. But respect, love, and caring for one another is what will make it last.

Sexual chemistry can be blinding. It's where you lose focus on the important things and are oblivious to the warning signs and red flags. It's important to remember that chemistry burns out over time. In fact, scientific studies have determined that chemistry usually lasts from a year and a half to three years. And then poof—it vanishes.

Our goal is for you to get past the specific first dates and to look *beyond* the chemistry. We want him to get to know you, and vice versa. This willingness to embark on a deeper exploration makes for a better chance for a deeper connection.

Dating today seems like a job interview, where you're

filtering information in and out. Dating shouldn't be a cold, unfeeling job interview. Too often we risk the danger of filtering out or being filtered out—with not enough information.

Knowing the difference between bad habits and bad character is essential. We want to steer you onto the road to a second date and to clearly understand the criteria for the job of being your life partner. This will allow for a broader look for the both of you. After the first few dates, you can begin to peek into exploring the possibility of compatibility.

We Want Full Acceptance—So Give It

For many women, love is a one-way street. The truth is that we want to be completely accepted by a man for who we are. But we're unwilling to accept him completely for who he is.

It's not about selling yourself short through compromise. It's about acceptance. It starts with you: your self-acceptance and self-love.

Several of our clients question this attitude. They ask: Why should I lower my standards? Why settle for ordinary? Some of our female clients complain that everyone is so needy, or neurotic, or picky, or negative, or immature, or critical, or controlling, or selfish, and on and on. This is often what psychologists call projection. As they say, if you wake up in the morning and each day you find people difficult—then hey, it happens. But if you keep meeting difficult people all day, day after day, month after month . . . time to look in the mirror!

What's the advantage of changing your current standards?

Well, you're single and you're reading this book. On another note, our female clients ask, why do I have to change? You want better luck and chances on the dating scene, don't you? So you need to change the formula you have been following until now.

Men are not asking for advice or searching for what they need to have a wonderful marriage. They are looking for what *feels* good to them. They don't want to change. To succeed in dating, many women need to consider a new strategy and approach.

But if you stick to the same old attitude, how can you expect new results?

Sometimes it's just a matter of looking within. You should know that often what we see in others is actually the story we are telling ourselves about them. We call these preconceived notions. These notions determine the lens through which we view our potential mates.

We have the luxury in our business of speaking to both the men and women. We know how their motors run. We advise our clients to drop the preconceived notions, scrutinize their wish list carefully, and be more realistic. We urge them to look at the positives in their date and to move forward to a second meeting.

Broadening Your Lens

Again, broaden your lenses so you can move from focusing on what he's not offering to feeling appreciation for what he is bringing to the table. We often tend to look at a quick snapshot of someone, like their online profile or a dinner, and fill in the blanks of what he and his life story would probably be. We make inaccurate assumptions based on a snippet of information.

Now on to a scientific study that addresses these preconceived notions.

Preconceived Notions and the MIT Dating Study

MIT examined this very concept scientifically. They divided two groups of singles into Groups A and B. In Group A each single was given only a first name, and in Group B each single was given a lot of information: age, location, career, pictures, marital history, children, religion, and so on. They were each sent out on one specific date.

Results? Group A was very successful in dating and most continued seeing their match, but Group B was very unsuccessful. Why?

The scientists derived that the reason Group B was very unsuccessful was because the singles had unrealistic preconceived notions and expectations prior to going out. They had already filled in the blanks and made a determination of what was right or wrong with the date prior to meeting them. In other words, they had already lost the game before they went up to bat! Such judgments usually come from preconceived notions from our past. We ignore the logic that such notions are not a good barometer of what may work in the future.

Sure, we are disappointed when someone doesn't meet our positive expectations. We're disappointed when they meet our negative assumptions. This dynamic is something we all do to save time. It's called heuristics. It's a shortcut to make decisions and make our lives easier.

We make judgments quickly in order to be more efficient. This strategy shortens decision-making time and allows us to function without constantly stopping to think about our next course of action. But sometimes—in fact, a lot of times—these strategies backfire on us, because they are outdated and inaccurate in the here and now.

Perfect Is the Enemy of Good

Before you summarily discard your first date, make a list of his positives. One thing we know from our 30-plus years of consulting and matchmaking is that there is no Mr. Perfect—or Ms. Perfect—and searching for perfect creates anxiety, disappointment, and lifelong dissatisfaction. If we keep looking for the absolute best in this dating marketplace, always looking over his shoulder to see if there's anyone better, wondering "Is this the best I can do?," we may miss someone wonderful because we didn't give him a second look or because our expectations were from an old laundry list.

It's moving from thinking "Is this the best I can do?" to rather: "Am I enjoying my time, and how do I feel when I'm with him?" It's moving from the judgmental brain to the contented heart.

In the end, what matters is finding someone who has the qualities you're seeking, someone who has enough of your must-haves as opposed to searching for someone who has everything.

Our matchmaking advice: go on a second date, just to be sure! Remember to let him pursue you by either calling or texting you first. When he does, lean back with warmth and kindness—give it some space. Breathe—whether he reaches out or not. Focus on other things in your life. If that second date ends up happening, think of it as an opportunity. We'll talk about this in more detail in the next chapter.

Summary

- Remember that chemistry is temporary and can be blinding—look for compatibility, for what's sustainable in the long run.
- Have you searched for the positives and not the negatives? You want acceptance too, so don't forget to give it!
- Be aware of the difference between bad habits and character flaws: habits can be changed, but character flaws can't.
- Don't forget that perfect isn't realistic. You don't want to forego a good match because of outdated or superficial expectations.

Chapter 8

The First *Real* Date (Hint: It's the Second)

In this chapter:

- How and what to share with him when you embark on that second date—keeping it light and positive while getting to know him better.
- How to suspend critical judgment—and also watch how he treats you and others.
- Tips for flirting (or a refresher!), and why it's better to wait to get physical.

Dietitian Bonnie was so excited when Matthew asked her out again. The first date had gone super well, and she really liked him. He met so many of her realistic needs and wants: smart, funny, good values, nice family.

Looking back, she realized she had been slightly awkward on the first date, afraid that he wasn't going to like her. She felt uptight. This time Bonnie made up her mind that she was going to relax and enjoy the date. She promised herself not to indulge her usual pattern, which was to be overly anxious or excessively available. By laying back just a little, while at the same time showing interest, Bonnie was laying the groundwork to guarantee more dates. She vowed to progress with ease from date two to three to four, in a relaxed and comfortable manner. And it worked! By demonstrating a positive and accepting attitude (as opposed to seeming needy), both Bonnie and Matthew enjoyed their second date tremendously.

Remember: Lean In *and* Lean Back

Don't forget: you want to keep a little mystery at the beginning of your relationship. It's not your job to be a completely open book; in fact, it's not a good idea to disclose too much at the beginning of the relationship, and definitely not a good idea to be clingy.

When a man is engaged with you, he will want more. He's a hunter and you have stirred his interest. He will want to see you, pursue you, and date you. So far, so good!

However, our research and scientific evidence reveal the fact that absence does make the heart grow fonder, especially when he's really into you. That's why your best move is to lean back a little (which we've discussed before). It's a delicate balance between being too available and playing hard to get. Make sure he knows you're interested, but don't fall all over him.

We're not saying to be dishonest, but we are saying this: save the intimate personal information about you, your family, finances, exes, and children. Men feel overwhelmed by too much disclosure too soon. They want to get to know you slowly, just like they disclose parts of themselves and their inner lives bit by bit, over time. If you share too much information up front, he may feel trapped or overwhelmed. Keep your personal life close to your chest, and choose to unveil details slowly as you get to know him better.

Let Him Set the Pace

Remember, the man in the dating pool is not your girlfriend. He's a guy—and they open up much more slowly. As the relationship unfolds and deepens, over several dates, that's the best time to begin to self-disclose about family life, about children, about career goals, about dreams, and about past hurts. The second date is *not* the time. If you're unsure when to spring the heavy stuff, do this: *mirror what he does*. Just make sure that you don't jump in too fast, because he'll run away, and you'll be dining at a table for one.

Studies have shown that as the relationship becomes closer and both begin to share personal information, the feelings deepen. Your date has to be self-disclosing too. Men are slower, so take your lead from him. It's also not how *much* you reveal, but *what* you reveal.

So, what can you discuss?

Here are our insider tips. Remember to share the positive up front. Lead with a smile and upbeat information. Only after the relationship develops and deepens should you decide it's time to share the struggles and difficulties of your life. You never know what the other person is reading into what you say. So carefully choose your topics and how much you disclose.

So your first date was light, fun, breezy. Now, as you enter the second date, pay attention to the subtleties in his personality, and his words. Observe the conversation and remember to keep it smooth.

If he's the silent type, don't panic and turn into a chatterbox to fill the quiet space. That's nerve-racking for both of you. Just try to relax. Perhaps you could arrive with some preselected topics and questions that will help him open up. Don't make the mistake of filling the awkward silences with personal hardship stories, or you'll sabotage any further chances with him. It takes confidence to sit through silences. But sometimes sitting silently can speak volumes!

Our client Julia is an oil painter and still very youthful looking at 52. She's truly a femme fatale. Her dates tend to fall all over her. How does Julia respond? Her reaction is to play very hard to get by taking days to answer texts or calls.

Such was the case when we introduced her to Scott, an art dealer in his late 40s. Like so many of the other gentlemen we set her up with, Scott was immediately smitten. They had a great date at a seafood restaurant on the intercoastal. They enjoyed sharing stories about work and clients, and laughed a lot.

And Scott called Julia for that second date. No response, so he called again a couple of days later. Still, Julia was playing it cool—deciding that absence makes the heart grow fonder. Puzzled, Scott called us to ask: "What's going on?" We pleaded ignorance—but then called Julia. She told us how she was playing it cool.

Repeatedly, we tried to explain to Julia that the way she was treating men wasn't working, and that she was jeopardizing her second date with Scott. But to no avail. Frustrated with Julia's ongoing lack of response, he stopped calling and decided to move on. Her erroneous strategy cost her a second date with a man she really liked. She lost what could have been a very sweet relationship. When leaning back becomes playing games, men sense it, and they realize they don't need the aggravation, no matter how attractive a woman may be.

Let's be very clear about our advice: when we say lean back, we're not talking about leaning *way* back. Just allow a little time to pass after he calls before responding—even just a few hours. Leave a little mystery. Also, it sends the message that you have a life and are not sitting by the phone waiting for his call. But don't leave days between his call and your answer. If you wait too long, it sends the message that you're just not interested. And if you are, by that time, he's not.

Talk the Talk

If you still feel a little nervous, don't worry. After all, he probably does too. Try to turn that nervous feeling (which feels like high school dating) into genuine excitement.

If you were a good listener and showed interest in your date, that's a recipe for success. Therefore, he liked you enough to schedule a second date. This is the time to let go of the first-date jitters and to move into a little deeper conversation. Get a little more real—a bit personal. That being said, don't turn the second date into confession time. Keep the conversation breezy. Not too deep, not controversial, and only positive. There will be plenty of time to discuss the difficult times in your life, and life in general. But ladies, the second date is not the time for a heart-to-heart.

Feel free to answer personal questions with an easygoing "Oh, let's talk about that another time." Remember that just because he asks a question doesn't mean you have to answer. But be gentle and light (not defensive) and keep the conversation flowing. Remember to compliment him, his choice of restaurant, and so on—just as important on the second date as on the first!

Think Positively

There's a great exercise we advise our clients to do. We tell them to take inventory from the start. Look at all the effort your date has made. Think about what he may have gone through to take you out—the emotional risk, choosing the venue, making the reservation, paying—all in an attempt to set the right mood and try to please you. Let him please you, and let him know how much you appreciate his efforts.

Although it may not be your taste (or your choice, your desired location, food, etc.), it's wonderful if you can appreciate him for what he did right. Try not to generalize one behavior or one choice he made and assume it's the whole person. His goal is to make you like him, so forgive him if he makes a misstep. Most men are clueless.

When you speak with him, look in his eyes. Stay off your cell phone, unless there's an emergency—it's simply rude, and a major turnoff. Smile when he talks; ask about him and his life. Laugh at his stories. Make him feel interesting, accepted, appreciated. Let him feel how happy you are to be with him, how enthused. Even if you're not sure, you'll bring out the best in him. Let him shine. Then you'll start to see the real him. Trust us: thinking positively will make everything about your date and your life better!

Watch the Way He Treats You

Further, watch the way he treats you, and how he treats the waiters. Is he trying to please you, or is he self-focused? You can tell a lot about someone's character by the way he treats waiters, busboys, taxi drivers, and others who serve him. Meanwhile, does he make you feel safe and that you're being listened to? Is he interested in you and your life or in just telling you about himself and his accomplishments? If you drive in two separate cars, does he walk you to your car? Some things he does may just be because he's nervous, or he has bad habits—or it may reveal a lot about him.

On the second date, you can begin to screen him a little deeper. While we recommended not to dig too deeply or ask personally intrusive questions, you can still scratch beneath the surface a little. Men can be sensitive and somewhat insecure, so don't judge or criticize him. Nothing kills the mood more than challenging or belittling his opinions, beliefs, or values. (Would you want him to do that to you?) You may decide to not go out again, but he's doing the best he can. So try to be kind—whether this is the only date or the beginning of a beautiful relationship. A positive disposition can turn a bad date into a great date!

Suspend Critical Judgment

A key strategy to employ on a second date is to make a point of reeling in your judgmental mindset. If you find yourself trying to rule him out because of x and y . . . try a little harder to wait until after the date to look at the pros and cons.

Research has shown that when we look for the positives, we find them. It's a confirmed psychological principle that if we open up, we can change our rigid and habitual ways of thinking. It may feel safer to continue the way we have always been, rather than opening up to other ways of thinking and judging. Remember, *if we do what we have always done, then our past will become our future*. We will find ourselves drowning in repetitious habits. If that's working for you, by all means carry on. If you're finding that it's a dead end, then try to create a new opportunity for potential dating and romance success.

Here's a suggestion to allow for a new perspective: look at your feelings floating by. A host of feelings are happening in us at all times. Look at your feelings as many fish swimming around together. Instead of grabbing on to one feeling, one fish, and committing to that one, just be a bystander.

Happy, sad, kind, selfish, worried, nervous, angry, critical, scared, insecure, excited, confident, loving, relaxed. There are many feelings swimming around. Don't grab on to any one. Instead, watch your feelings lazily swimming by. Let them swim by. Just watch them and relax. You're just observing.

Flirting for Beginners—or a Refresher Course

Even if he's not for you or you're not into him, use this date as a practice session. This is a good time to practice relating and flirting—when the stakes are not so high.

What does that look like? Maintain good eye contact with a softened gaze. By this we mean softening your eyes, almost looking at him with a gauze filter. It's less harsh, less piercing.

Physically lean in, if you're comfortable, because it shows interest. It's okay to touch his hand once or twice during dinner, very lightly and quickly. Compliment him when he talks about something that clearly interests him. Practice saying things like: "Oh, that sounds great," or "Wow you work so hard," or "Sounds like you're a great friend, son, brother, father," or "I really love your attitude," or "You look so happy when you talk about x, that's such an interesting way to think about it."

You can plan some topics to discuss before you go on your second date. Try to bring up happy subjects and topics, such as what he loves to do for fun, what's on his bucket list, where he wants to travel, what's the best trip he ever went on, where he grew up, whether he has sisters and brothers. Best to stay away from the controversial ones (politics, money) and to continue to talk breezily and touch lightly with a little more information-gathering.

During the date, don't mention or hint at seeing him again. Yes, a man can smell neediness. He's still the pursuer, so let him pursue.

Physical Intimacy: When Is It Right?

It's a very important topic and important to remember: physical intimacy is great, but at the right time. Having sex prematurely is a relationship killer.

We are going to repeat this: *having sex prematurely is a relationship killer.*

Men don't respect women who sleep with them too soon. And yes, the second date is too soon. In fact, if there is not an emotional connection regardless of the number of dates, it's too soon.

Our rule of thumb is: if you feel comfortable being emotionally naked, then physical nakedness is fine.

We have found that after having sex the relationship moves to a different level—but none of it is good if the relationship is not ready. Men and women put each other under a microscope after physical intimacy that neither may be ready for. Premature sex may cloud your judgment, even keep you in a dysfunctional situation for a while or end the affair. So take your time—once you jump off the diving board, you're in up to your neck!

DON'T BE PHYSICALLY NAKED UNTIL YOU'RE READY TO BE EMOTIONALLY NAKED.

A Minor Shift: Sara's Case

Having a successful second date had been particularly challenging for our client Sara—so much so that she never made it to a third date with anyone. She struggled with the dilemma of showing too much or too little interest, fearing that the wrong move could scare any man off, and it often did. So her default position was to act like an ice princess, cold and distant.

With a lot of coaching, Sara decided to approach her second date a little differently. She went out with Ben, a software engineer, to a frozen yogurt shop where you make your own dessert creations. He wore a sports jacket, and his chestnut hair fell jauntily into his eyes. She liked his self-assured quiet demeanor. This time she was warm, affectionate, appreciative, and even a little flirty with a warm hand touch.

She focused on Ben's positive traits and behaviors, mentally putting him in the friend zone without agonizing whether or not she was saying the right thing. She didn't obsess over whether he liked her or not—and it made all the difference!

When Ben asked her out for a third date in the middle of dinner, she was shocked at how such a small shift in her attitude could result in such a positive outcome. We, as her matchmakers, were thrilled with her success. Bravo to Sara!

Summary

- Think positive and keep your critical judgments at bay—give him a chance (and yourself)!
- Remember that he's not your girlfriend; don't overshare.
- Flirt and have fun—but keep it light, and don't jump into physical intimacy too soon.
- Keep in mind that minor shifts in your attitude can achieve significant results.

Chapter 9

What Next? Date Analysis and Relationship-Readiness

In this chapter:

- How to figure out if you're relationship-ready: unloading emotional baggage and making changes for the positive.
- How to figure out if *he's* relationship-ready: the signs to look for that tell you he is.
- Tips for determining your attachment style and watching his love language.

Laura, a nursery-school teacher and a longtime divorcée, was a nurturing, self-sufficient woman who had a steady and quiet life. But she found herself at home alone too often at night, watching romantic films like *Sleepless in Seattle*—rather than getting out there to have another chance at her own happiness. But then she tried an online dating app, after several friends convinced her that life could be more than Tom Hanks and Meg Ryan.

The first week on the dating app, Laura met her share of creeps and drips—men with no boundaries, or men who were looking for surrogate mothers. But she was a big girl and handled the aggravation quickly and firmly. And it didn't discourage her. At the same time, Laura was on a diet—those movie nights at home had involved lots of snacking—and the mirror was telling her that she looked better than ever. About two weeks into her dating app adventure, Laura found Jake online. Boyishly handsome, tall, a tennis buff with an adorable John Krasinski vibe, Jake was intriguing. He was divorced and dating casually, but managed a music store that dominated his days.

Laura wanted to know more about Jake. After a few days of online chat, they moved to the phone. That was equally delightful. Then he asked her to get together for coffee. When they met, it was evident that sparks were flying. He was funny, sweetly self-confident, and appealing. A Thai dinner was their second date, and the conversation flowed on both sides. It was effortless, like breathing. Laura was encouraged.

Oddly, it took a couple of weeks for them to have their next date, which was a Sunday afternoon at a local gallery. Laura wondered whether Jake was cooling off. He called and explained that he really liked her, but told her that his mother, Myrna, lived in an assisted-living facility nearby. While she was an active octogenarian, involved in mahjong and Pilates, the platinum-haired Myrna liked to see her son—several times a week. That made it tough to coordinate his schedule, he admitted. As soon as he closed the music store, he often had plans for dinner with her, or she had an errand for him or needed help with a burnt-out light bulb in her bathroom. Myrna had wanted Jake to move into her facility, but he wasn't old enough to qualify (not that he wanted to!).

After Jake postponed the third and fourth dates, Laura was not happy. Sure, he was profuse with apologies and explained that his mother needed him for one thing or another. But Laura soon realized that there was another woman in this relationship—and she wasn't going to let go. Nor did Jake seem like he was in a rush to establish better boundaries with his mother so that he could be free to go out on dates. He said he felt guilty about the situation but that there was a complicated backstory. He explained that his father had died soon after his bar mitzvah, and he had grown up with his mother depending on him as the man of the house, since she had two younger daughters.

Laura understood and reassured Jake that she was willing to be patient, but the situation upset her- and she found herself back on the couch, eating ice cream and watching romantic comedies. While Laura was impressed with Jake's loyalty to Myrna and his emotional generosity, the scenario pushed her buttons fiercely.

You see, Laura's first husband, Joshua, had had a complicated relationship with his mother. That is, she was clingy—and didn't like Laura all that much, a fact that she was not shy about making clear. Over the course of their 10-year marriage, Laura was always competing with her mother-in-law for time with her own husband. The fact that Joshua's mother moved two blocks from Joshua's home was the first tip-off. Matters only escalated over the years. Laura didn't have the nerve to tell her mother-in-law to back off, thinking it was her husband's place to correct the situation. But Joshua, assertive in his corporate world, had an Achilles heel—and it was letting his mother run his life.

The situation with Jake was a flashback to the three-way marriage she had had with Joshua. And the warning signs were already there. Laura was more mature now, and more likely to assert herself. But she had only known Jake for two months; was it premature to read him the riot act? Would he accuse her of being pushy? Would he feel threatened? Once she said her piece, he might resent her and break it off. And she didn't want to lose this sweet and gentle man. But he was a mama's boy—at age 47! What to do?

Are You Relationship-Ready?

At this point in your dating efforts, it's common that old emotional baggage starts to surface. After all, we are humans with long memories and long pasts. And old habits are hard to break.

Unloading Emotional Baggage

Baggage? What does that mean, and what does that look like? Pay attention to the story you're telling yourself about your date—even before meeting him. Are there some negative notions already running in your head? It's important to take a break and be an outside observer to your internal monologue. What are your internal voices saying? To be cautious? Guarded? Pessimistic? Negative? Mistrustful? I'm too fat; I'm too old; I can't wait; I feel excited; I feel confident; and so on.

Most important question: Are you relationship-ready? That is, are you ready to enter the dating pool again? If you're struggling with past relationship blues, or caught in old habits, or hanging on to one idea of the ideal man, or comparing the new date to your old love, then you have emotional baggage. Yep! And trust us, it's going to interfere with your chances for happily ever after.

That is, unless you do the work and unload the baggage.

If you feel stuck, here are questions to consider:

- Are you still working through an old relationship?
- When you think of that past relationship, what feelings does it bring up?
- Ask yourself honestly: What made that relationship work? What made it fail?
- How much did you feel you contributed to its demise? In what way?
- What strengths did you bring to the relationship?
- What were your weaknesses?

DON'T BRING YOUR EX ON YOUR NEW DATE.

If you're looking back at your past relationship with rose-colored glasses or with lots of self-blame, we have news for you: this is real evidence that you have emotional baggage.

Now is the time to look into resolving your past. Will it affect your present and future possibilities of a happy relationship?

As lonely or in need of companionship as you may feel, moving forward too quickly may backfire. When you have worked through the steps—sadness, anger, acceptance, and resolution—you will feel it, and it will energize you. It's hard to carry heavy weights for a long time. Our goal for you is to neutralize the overpowering memories of your past relationship so that you're open to exploring new possibilities. The past belongs in the past—not intruding into your present and future.

Once you free yourself of your past baggage, you'll be open to exploring new relationships and new opportunities with an open mind and heart. This is the true definition of being relationship-ready!

We understand the reluctance. When exposed to changing our routines, habits, preferences, behaviors, and choices, we often resist. Sometimes change doesn't feel good, but it's necessary for us to grow. It's human nature to repeat old patterns and stay inside our comfort zone. It seems safe and secure to repeat what's familiar. While this appears to be true, we then miss out on the new and the different—where there are possibilities of a great relationship. Remind yourself that it's human nature to resist change but life-enhancing when you grow as a person.

Please pay particular attention if we push your buttons in this chapter. Resolving emotional baggage is hard work. It's very likely that if you're extra sensitive about a particular issue, it's probably because we hit a nerve. Our intention is not to hurt, but to comfort. Your emotional baggage is in reality old wounds that need to be acknowledged, explored, and healed.

We all desire to improve our chances of finding a happy, fulfilling relationship. But many of us just don't know how. Here are a few ideas that may help with the exploration of your habits, patterns, and behaviors in order to make better and healthier choices in choosing a partner (further resources in the Appendix).

Please understand, readers: we don't want to offend or lose you! If our advice bruises you, here's what to do. Put down this book for a day and think about the issues we covered. Think about your needs and your past. Take a deep breath. If you find that our advice occasionally hurts, then you know we are on the right track! And we will see this through together.

If what you're doing is working for you, then please disregard our advice.

We are on your side throughout this process. But sometimes we need to shine a light on your blind spots. If you're willing to look, we encourage you to do so, because it will be ultimately rewarding. We only want to enhance, empower, and enrich your love life. That way you can have the relationship of your dreams.

Ch-Ch-Changes

Start by making a short list of some things you'd like to change in yourself. We find that women usually judge themselves pretty harshly. This is not about that; this is about changing one habit that will start the ball rolling in a different direction. If you know that making changes will be good for you but don't feel you know how, just try out one new behavior. If you practice it long enough, it will no longer be an act—it will be part of the new and improved you.

Choose one thing that's pretty easy to incorporate into your routine. For example: walking briskly for 15 minutes a day, reading an article from a very different point of view than yours, making a list of three things you're grateful for each day, repeating two affirmations a day.

Some examples of affirmations:

- "I love and approve of myself."

- "I trust life will bring me to my highest good."
- "I deserve the best and accept it now."
- "All is well."
- "Things generally work out."
- "I'm loving where I am right now and am eager for new changes."

Research suggests that just changing one thing may start a ripple effect. Then a wave begins that will open new ways of screening, choosing, relating, and committing. This brings you closer to starting a new chapter of happily ever after.

Preparing for a Third Date

So now you have a decision to make: Do you want to move forward to a third date? Again, we suggest you look at the essentials of your prospective partner: his character, values, goals, cultural similarities. Look at the examples of compatibility. Other essentials for consideration may include religion or politics.

Being Picky

As you assess his strengths and weaknesses, we offer one major flag of caution: if you're disqualifying this man because of his height, the color of his hair or eyes, the way he dresses, his dietary food choices, or his weight (significant health risks aside), then you should examine yourself very carefully—because you're rejecting someone for something that's nonessential and not crucial. Is this a way to avoid closeness? If so, some soul-searching is advised, for some of these are nonessentials and can easily be changed.

Remember, habits can be changed; character flaws can't. Before you toss him to the wind, separate your preferences (wants) from your essentials (needs). And remember that while chemistry can grow, it can also diminish. Connection and compatibility are the essence of a long-term, happy, and successful relationship. While no one person has everything, when you're finally in the right relationship, you'll find it as easy as walking in a comfortable pair of shoes.

Attachment Style and Love Language

Exploring your love language and attachment style is a way to learn about your inner psyche. They can be eye-openers, a way to shine a light on your individual needs. These are synopsized here.

The Five Love Languages by Gary Chapman unlocks the door to understanding essentially what you need in a partner and vice versa. The five love languages are words of affection, quality time, receiving gifts, acts of service, and physical touch. To discover which language is basic to your emotional health is paramount to receiving the love that you need and want. Read this book—it's awesome!

Attached by Amir Levine and Rachel Heller is a scientific book that touches on the innermost core of people's lives. Our attachment style varies depending on our upbringing, how our parents cared for us, and our life experiences. The three attachment styles are anxious, avoidant, and secure. Here is essential information to understand how we feel when dating and mating based on our attachment style, and how we can navigate the dating trenches with clarity.

Other essentials from various experts are discussed and referenced in our Appendix.

Many of our clients tell us, "I just attract the wrong men." We say, maybe you're accepting the wrong men or unconsciously repeating old, dysfunctional patterns. Bringing them to a conscious level can help you change that pattern once and for all.

It's when we are wading or diving into the dating pool that the old patterns and skeletons will begin to emerge. Pay close attention and commit yourself to adjusting and changing as needed. Examine yourself and determine what's stopping you from being a loving partner—and having a loving partner.

Is He Relationship-Ready?

What does that mean?

It means: either he resolved *his* emotional baggage and is ready for a serious loving relationship, or he is loving his single life and not ready for a committed relationship.

How do you recognize a man who's relationship-ready?

A man who is relationship-ready is interested in meeting and exploring the possibilities of a woman as a life partner.

What sets him apart is that he's truly interested in getting to know you and in sharing who he is with you.

He stays in touch between dates. He makes you a priority. He doesn't avoid or delay dates. He moves mountains to see you. He doesn't set up roadblocks, and never intentionally keeps you guessing.

He wants to know about you, your life, and your family. He's looking ahead with confidence, so he makes future plans with you. He asks for your input and advice. These are great signs. Once you move into the third date, be open. Stay interested in learning about him. Keep stories about yourself upbeat, and don't drone on and on. But when you do share them, hopefully he doesn't immediately change the topic back to himself.

That being said, give him a chance to shine. And let him know you're enjoying him.

The relationship-ready man has the openness, ease, and self-confidence to pursue you. So keep the lines of communication open! Send the right signals, and he will be drawn to you. Bring your compassion, authenticity, and kindness to every date.

Follow His Lead: But Pay Attention to Your Gut

Let him continue to be the director of this show. Pay attention to how he treats you and how you feel when you're with him. If you're in touch with your gut feelings without all the mental chatter, then listen to your gut. Believe what he says. We often are swayed by chemistry. Therefore, we foolishly ignore our instincts and, even worse, ignore the signals this man is sending.

When we are attracted to him, we make excuses and disregard red flags. You have no time to waste—so don't! As they say, when someone is showing you who they are—believe them.

Is He Projecting His Past on to You?

Of course he is! We're all products of our past, especially our childhood. Here is a shocker: the way we date tends to replicate the relationship we had with our opposite-sex parent. In this case, we are discussing how men see you through the veil of his relationship with his mother.

For you, it's how you look at men you're dating through the veil of how you saw, felt, heard, and reacted on a deep level to your father. Here we will focus on your date. Pay attention when he talks about his mother. How does he feel about her? Listen to details about how he treats her and how she treated him. This is generally a sign of how he feels about women in general.

Does he see his mother as controlling, needy, hard to please, passive, or dependent? This will often get projected onto the women he meets. It will determine how he treats and feels about them. An oversensitivity to whatever his feelings were when he was being raised will often be played out subconsciously toward you. Frequently, the way he reacts toward you is linked with how he reacted toward his parents, and especially his mother, in the past. He may have been drawn toward his parents or forced to throw up a defense. So watch and listen closely and understand what he is revealing about himself, because it will ultimately affect how he treats you.

Summary

- Learn about your love language and attachment style.
- Be proactive in determining past relationship patterns that aren't helping you anymore—time to let them go!
- Remember that there's a difference between being picky and listening to your true gut instincts.
- Keep in mind that change isn't easy—but personal growth is rewarding.
- Don't forget that *both* of you need to be relationship-ready in order to move forward!
- Pay attention to his love language to see what it is.

Chapter 10

Opening Your Mind and Heart

In this chapter:

- Understanding why we respond the way we do when something happens on a date.
- How to understand cognitive behavioral therapy by using a simple model for change.
- Tips for neutralizing the negative and accentuating the positive.

In our meetings with clients, we advise that they learn to open their minds as a prelude to opening their hearts.

This advice is usually met with a puzzled look. Clients ask us to explain. So we do.

Studies show that many women are held back by old ideas based on unpleasant past experiences. In fact, many women in the dating pool are shortchanging, sabotaging, and narrowing their possibilities of connecting to someone new.

While experience is a good teacher, it's not always the best. The past is the past; it can have limited or negative value in the here and now. Every day is a new experience and should be met with a new frame of mind. That means dropping longstanding prejudices, fears, and negativity that are sabotaging you and your dates.

While it sounds simple, it's a complicated dynamic. Let us explain a bit further.

Most of us are accustomed to believing that external circumstances define and determine our mindsets. That is, we think we are simply reacting to the events, situations, and behavior of others that we encounter on our journey through life. This is a myth we wish to dispel.

Consider this dating scenario that a client of ours related to us.

Kim was a sweet divorcée who ran a small independent bookstore. She enjoyed cooking, jogging, and of course, reading. She was in good shape and looked 10 years younger than her age of 52. Being single was a lot better than her disastrous five years with Hank, an egotistical and emotionally withholding car dealer. Kim came to us because she was ready to take a chance on romance. We began finding her matches.

Kim happily went on a first date with Arnie, a copywriter at a small local ad agency. But when he took a business phone call 20 minutes into their lunch, she got up and stormed out of the restaurant, leaving Arnie sitting there in shock. And then there was Luke, a man who ran a health club. He was buff and handsome. But he didn't stand up when Kim walked into the coffee shop, like she expected of a gentleman. She felt immediately insulted. At that point Kim shut down coldly and, after conversing for an hour, excused herself and left.

What was going on here?

We talked seriously and sympathetically to Kim, who felt she was justified in ending both dates because of perceived rudeness. After 15 minutes of conversation, she finally got to the truth of the situation: the behavior of Arnie and Luke seemed selfish to her, and she immediately flashed back to her boorish ex-husband Hank. That scared her and caused her to close down and flee. Kim was holding on to negative past experiences and using them to guide her through dating, often acting impulsively. And this mindset was sabotaging her dates.

We explained to her what was going on. She was shocked at how bad memories were jeopardizing her current chances at happiness.

We tell all clients that there are bound to be rough moments on a first date. The impulse is to react strongly. But before passing judgment and becoming hurt, upset, mad, or unhappy, it's instructive to evaluate your own responses. You will learn something about yourself. We tell clients about the value of looking behind their own reactions in order to explore their thoughts and assumptions. There's a good chance that your actions are being guided by internal statements that you are not even aware of. In Kim's case, the internal statement was "No one is ever going to ignore me like that darn Hank. I'll dump him before being treated like that again."

Kim's defensiveness kept coming up on her first dates—and you see how they turned out. She took the casual actions of her dates personally, and cut them off. She didn't ask herself *why* she was reacting so dramatically and so angrily. She didn't give the men a chance to defend or explain themselves. Often these thoughts from the past lead us to decide that the current date is not a viable candidate. We tell ourselves, based on those inner statements, that he's not worthy of a second look—and we summarily discount or dismiss him.

Each date and each person is a unique individual. Just because they may have a similar trait to someone in your past doesn't make them the same as that person. Dismissing people out of hand because of that misconception is a losing strategy.

That attitude didn't work for Kim. And it won't work for you. Do yourself a favor and take inventory of your internal statements. Then ask yourself if they are going to help or hinder your efforts on the dating scene.

Why Do We Respond the Way We Do?

Let's stop and look a little deeper. What really makes us respond the way we do? It's not the situation, action, or words of another person. Rather, it's how we perceive and *think* about that person or that action that has affected us. Our thoughts or beliefs trigger our emotions and our actions. This is the basis of cognitive therapy. That is the phenomenon where old patterns and rigid ways of thinking are limiting your possibilities of finding suitable partners in the present.

This is why we advise our clients to just *observe* their thoughts, and see if they're based on accurate assumptions or conclusions. We tell our clients with certainty that we know if they can change their thoughts—that is, open their minds—then they will successfully change their emotions and open their hearts. Trust us: by changing your thoughts and thus your resultant feelings, you will change the outcome of your date—for the better.

This is the basis of a technique we'd like to share with you. We've helped hundreds of people open up their minds and then their hearts. The result is that you will explore new potential relationships with a fresh set of lenses. That's the scientific dynamic behind cognitive behavioral therapy.

How You Think Affects How You Feel

Cognitive therapy is based on the theory that the way each of us *feels* is largely determined by how we *think* about the world, people, events. This specific automatic thinking originates from your previous experiences—usually created as a defensive and protective strategy, to keep you safe. But this negative thinking is holding you back!

We advise clients to be open-minded when exploring new possibilities for a potential relationship. We ask them to suspend automatic critical judgment. But how can you turn off that negative inner voice or thinking?

Here's a step-by-step guide to follow based on cognitive behavioral therapy:

1. Try to identify the thoughts and judgments you're making that are prompting your feelings. What set you off?

2. Recognize the link between your thoughts and the feelings that are triggered. How did you feel as a result of that thought? Good or bad?

3. If negative, try to neutralize the thought by substituting it with a nonemotional, nonjudgmental one. Example: *He didn't chew loudly to bug me; that's just his habit.*

4. Next, this will create a new feeling, instead of the old habitual response. Example: *Rather than getting angry when he takes a cell call, make the assumption that it's just a habit, not a character flaw.* So, rather than becoming enslaved to an attitude or emotion based on a past experience, decide to respond differently and more calmly with an open mind. For example, *I'm going to stay open to this and not listen to my automatic thought. I'll give him a chance!*

Remember that all thoughts and reactions can be changed. The trick is getting out of your comfort zone that is your habitual way of responding.

Neutralizing the Thought

Let's look at our dating examples from above and find ways to defuse the situations.

On their date, Arnie the copywriter answers a business phone call.

Here's a *neutralized thought* for Kim to pursue: Although Arnie answered his phone while we were eating, maybe it was an important call. Perhaps he has a sick relative or friend. Maybe he doesn't realize that it's hurtful to me to answer a call during our date. Maybe it's just a bad habit. My ex-husband Hank did that to me and was so thoughtless and insensitive. But Arnie didn't do this to push my buttons like Hank. Maybe Arnie really is not like my ex. Despite that phone call, Arnie has been polite throughout the date. So I'm going to change my internal statements this time. I'm going to let it go and see Arnie again.

On their date, Luke the health club owner doesn't stand up to greet Kim.

Here's a *neutralized thought* for Kim to pursue: Luke didn't stand up to greet me for several possible reasons: Maybe he was just tired. He's not formal. Maybe he hurt himself working out at the gym. Maybe he's nervous and forgot his manners. Perhaps his ex discouraged him from such formalities. Sure, my ex was impolite. But Luke is not my ex, and I shouldn't treat him like he is. Maybe I'm being oversensitive? Also, I liked the way he looked at me. Luke had good eye contact and was a gentleman throughout the evening. He cared about me and whether I was enjoying my dinner, and even poured my wine each time. I'll look for the good! Not standing up really is not a red flag. Maybe I shouldn't rule Luke out because of that behavior, here and now.

Simple Model for Change Explained

Cognitive behavioral therapy sounds complicated—but don't get scared off! Here is a simple model of the concept, explained in a nutshell.

An event happens on your date. Let's call this A.

You have a thought about the event on your date. Let's call this B.

Then you have a feeling in response to the thought about the event that happens on your date. Let's call that C.

It looks like this:

A (event) + B (thoughts) = C (feeling)

Look at the incident with Arnie the copywriter through your old rigid thinking:

A (he talked on the phone during our date)
+ B (how rude) = C (hurt)

OUR THOUGHTS, NOT EVENTS, CONTROL OUR FEELINGS.

Looking at this example of Arnie the copywriter with neutralized new thinking:

A (he talked on the phone)
+ B (maybe a bad habit) = C (soothed)

OUR THOUGHTS, NOT EVENTS, CONTROL OUR FEELINGS.

What changed here? It's all about thoughts and attitude. People often make the mistake of assuming that just because they're feeling something, it must be true. The only thing that changed in this first example is thought B. That is, the negative and judgmental thought became neutralized and more accepting. Often we are just not aware of our negative and reactive thoughts and beliefs because they're so automatic. They were probably created as self-protection at some point, and we react quickly without even being aware.

But they are there, and they affect not only the way we feel, but also the decisions we make and the way we act. All the time our brains are overanalyzing, turning over thoughts and ideas—and responding in a habitual way that hurts us and harms our date. These negative reactions based on internal statements happen quickly, and we're not accustomed to slowing them down. However, they play a key role in our emotions and, as a result, in the choices we make. It's crucial to bring them to a conscious level and to tame them. Our happily ever after depends on this positive change in our reactions.

Change Is Not Easy

Although it can be scary to suspend judgment, remember: it can also be enlightening and freeing. The only thing that keeps you stuck in the past are your habitual ways of thinking and responding. These old negative habits are not serving you, and they certainly won't improve your chances on the dating scene!

Here are some questions to think about to avoid jumping to conclusions:

- Was my reaction in proportion to the incident? Did I overreact?
- How did I make him feel? How did I feel?
- Are these feelings based on the present reality, or on a past hurt?
- What's the evidence for my judgmental conclusion? Is it based on old automatic thinking?
- Do my judgments give me a feeling of safety? Is this a way to protect myself?
- Do I need to build some deeper self-understanding, self-esteem, and self-worth?
- What will I lose if I remain open-minded?

Summary

- Be ready to open your mind—your heart will follow!
- Remember that the way you think has a direct impact on the way you feel: assume the negative and you'll find it, but expect the positive, and that's what you'll see instead.
- Don't beat yourself up for finding change difficult—it is! But you can do it, a step at a time.
- Imagine the positive outcomes in your dating future if you give both you and your date the benefit of the doubt.

Chapter 11

Getting Out of Your Comfort Zone

In this chapter:

- How your inner thoughts directly affect the way you view yourself, and how you operate in the world.
- Tips for developing your sense of self so that you feel steady and secure when you dive into that dating pool.
- Expanding your comfort zone—and why the risks are worth the reward.

Gail was an accomplished, Harvard-trained physician, world-renowned for her breakthroughs in eczema research and treatment. Brainy, she was also attractive, a rare thing of beauty among her colleagues. For Gail, it was an unexpected flowering: as a child, she was the youngest of four children and always in the shadow of her two sisters and older brother. Her siblings were popular, good-looking, and had lots of friends, but Gail was by nature a loner, and she was plain-looking. Thankfully, she had a flair for school. Her parents labeled Gail "the Smart One."

Dates were few for the brainy girl, who had a crippling shyness. She won several science fair awards in junior high and high school, but teen romance passed her by. She had a difficult time with small talk. Consequently, on the rare nights when Gail would go on a date, she would revert back to her role as the shy one—and frustrated boys would drop her off early and never call again.

When she began medical school, Gail excelled early and drew lots of positive attention. In the intervening years, she had grown into her looks and was now a quietly attractive woman. But she had zero confidence, still feeling she was a homely girl. When a classmate named Theodore began dating her seriously, Gail thought it was her only chance at romance. They were married within months, but the marriage turned out to be little more than a meeting of the minds. Theodore was more interested in test tubes than affection. Within a year, Gail had divorced her cold husband, transferred to another medical school, and put the pieces of her life back together. While revered by her professional colleagues and patients, by age 39 she was wary of ever finding another romance.

Gail was not only a professional visionary; she had social poise and charm to go along with her brains (she'd clearly grown out of her shyness, too). Therefore, she was often giving presentations on her research at conferences across the country and abroad. Her achievements afforded her great exposure, and she had many fans among her colleagues. But science was her day job, and Gail didn't want to tie the knot with a man from her own field after the travesty of her marriage to Theodore. She wanted a home life where she could take a break from talking science all the time.

Gail found her way to our matchmaking services. She was bright enough to understand what was holding her back in life, and brilliantly self-diagnosed herself in our first session together. Gail saw herself as a science experiment and wanted us to work our theories on her in an attempt to achieve a great transformation.

As our coaching began, we helped Gail revisit her past and the wounds that stemmed from her nerdy childhood as the shy and homely one. We helped her explore the survival tactics she had established to protect herself—but that also kept her at arm's length from any potential suitors. Through our weeks of counsel, we worked to empower Gail by helping her tear down long-held and unflattering impressions of herself. We helped her catalogue her many attributes and gave her permission to feel good about herself again.

The results were startling. She began to relax, laugh, and actually have a willingness to go out on dates. Accordingly, we introduced her to Jeff, 42, a branding expert at a high-profile regional marketing company. With equal amounts of excitement and doubt, Gail accepted Jeff's invitation for dinner at Luigi's, a family-style Italian restaurant with a retro décor theme: checkered tablecloths, Chianti bottles with candles on each table, huge portions, and a violinist who walked from table to table serenading the diners.

Gail was delighted by the campy but romantic atmosphere. And her chemistry with Jeff was immediate. Not only was he easygoing, with a flair for witty stories, but he had penetrating blue eyes and a muscular body from workouts in his home gym. Gail proved the perfect audience for Jeff's jokes. She felt herself open up in a way that she never had before. Talk about a chemical reaction! Within six months of steady dating, Gail told us that Jeff had taken her back to Luigi's and given her an engagement ring. The experiment, Gail announced in an exaggerated scientific voice, had been a success!

Effects of Inner Thoughts on Self-Esteem

We've discussed thoughts and how they negatively or inaccurately affect your feelings toward others.

Now we are broadening the topic to include how your thoughts affect your beliefs about yourself, including your self-concept, self-worth, and self-esteem—which are all different. Let us explain.

Age-old beliefs stem from comments passed on from parents, partners, employers, teachers, and friends. They have affected your past and present. If left unchanged, these forces will negatively impact your future—and destroy your dating chances.

GET RID OF YOUR DISTORTED SELF-IMAGE. AND EMBRACE THE BEAUTIFUL YOU.

It's the thought that counts. So first, recognize that the thoughts you're having right now are shaping your future.

But they're only thoughts, you say. What's the big deal?

So glad you asked! The truth is that thoughts can make or break your life. The good news is that negative thoughts that limit your potential can be changed right now.

Here are the steps to follow:

1. Understand the concepts.
2. Understand where thoughts come from, and listen to them.
3. Reprogram the automatic recording in your mind—or shut it off! (This step is the toughest.)
4. Use affirmations and exercises to develop self-esteem.
5. Reclaim your future.
6. Ready yourself to step outside your comfort zone. Why? Because comfort zones keep you stuck in the past. It's time to create a new future.

So what's the difference between self-concept, self-esteem, and self-worth?

These are all concepts in psychology referring to your perception of yourself. Your self-concept *includes* self-esteem and self-worth. Self-esteem is your overall perception of yourself in the outside world. Self-worth is your internal perception of your own worth.

Although self-esteem and self-worth are related to how a person views themselves, they apply to different aspects. Despite the fact that these terms are often used interchangeably, there is a major difference between them. Expanding on the definition above: self-esteem is the confidence a person has about their competence and their belief about their achievements in the world. Self-worth is how they feel about their innermost self—in other words, the value you place on your life. We see many examples of this in politics and the entertainment industry, where someone may seem to be supremely confident, almost swaggering, but inside feels they have little value. They spend their lives trying to prove their worth to others, desperately hoping to win approval.

Desperation is the last thing you want to convey. But when your self-esteem and self-worth are in alignment, you're anything but desperate; on the contrary, you're clearly more at ease and comfortable in your own skin.

An easy way to remember the distinction between self-esteem and self-worth is by thinking about self-esteem as the *outside* you—the person you are in the world, your capabilities—whereas self-worth is the *inside* you, your core self, or what we refer to as your *true self.*

If you have a healthy self-concept, self-worth, and self-esteem, that's good news. You will be more open to stepping out of your comfort zone and more confident about working to attain your goals and dreams.

These two concepts—self-esteem and self-worth—work together to make up your multifaceted self-concept. They determine how your interactions and attitude will affect your daily life.

Our self-esteem starts with our perception of our selves: namely, our physical, social, educational, moral, intellectual, and temperamental beliefs of self. Other dimensions that also affect what we believe about ourselves include age, gender, religion, social and economic status, and nationality.

Self-esteem is rarely all positive or all negative. A person may possess both positive and negative beliefs in different domains. (For example, a husband thinks of himself as a good father but sees his physical self as out of shape. Or a student thinks of herself as a great athlete, but she struggles academically.)

However your view of yourself is based on your belief rather than on fact. Your self-concept doesn't necessarily correspond with external reality. In fact, others may see you differently. They may actually have a higher opinion of you than you do yourself!

We can retain outdated ideas about ourselves from childhood—just like Gail did. For a long time she continued to see herself as plain and shy, even when she no longer was. Another example: an obese child may still see herself as overweight when she reaches adulthood, despite the fact that she's slim and in excellent shape.

But what you believe about yourself—good or bad—is *your* reality and will be a powerful factor in determining your behavior. If you believe you're inferior to others, you will probably act in a self-defeating fashion. If you believe you're strong and resilient, you will likely succeed, even against great odds.

In other words, your sense of self can help or hinder you.

Therefore, our self-esteem and worth is affected by how we feel about ourselves and how we judge our abilities, competencies, and worth as a person. When we put some effort into boosting these self-evaluations, our view of ourselves will adjust to accommodate these changes.

We have the ability to change how we think about ourselves by working on becoming more like our ideal selves. Then, we will be able to start to feel more stable and safer in our skin. We will be more likely to step outside our comfort zones and explore new possibilities—which is what dating is all about!

How to Develop Self-Worth

Who are you? How do you feel about yourself?

Better yet, do you have an answer?

Why is self-worth important? We view the world through the lens of our self-worth; the quality of our lives is vastly impacted by how we feel about our innermost true self. What we do know for certain is that anyone, at any age or stage of their life, can build healthy self-worth, no matter what they've endured.

We are all the result of external messages and events. On top of that, we create an internal reaction to those events that further defines our personality.

So who are you? Who's the authentic, real you deep inside?

Are you just reacting to messages from the past? Has that made you feel insecure, anxious, sad, lonely, and unworthy, or happy, loved, capable, and lovable? As we explained, we tend to re-create the relationships from our family of origin in our personal relationships.

Which brings us to a big question: How can we change the old messages that we are playing in our minds and develop a different mindset? How do we grow and foster self-esteem and self-worth now?

Remember, our thoughts control our feelings, and this relates to our self-esteem and self-worth. Sometimes the old patterns of thought—that negative, critical, judgmental voice in our heads—are on automatic pilot.

I invite you to step off the plane. Right now. Instead, listen closely to the messages you're telling yourself about yourself.

Listen carefully. Write them down. Make a list.

Whose voice is this? Try to remember where, when, and who sent those messages to you.

Usually it's somebody from long ago and far away who planted those ideas in our heads. Another person's opinions that we integrated. Another person's critical messages that invaded our consciousness and undermined or enhanced our sense of self-worth.

Take some time to review this list. Say the ideas aloud. That may help you remember where you heard them first. You will probably have an *aha* moment where you realize: "So that's where that idea or judgment came from!"

Stepping from the Past into the Present

Once you have identified the thoughts and feelings that influence how you view and feel about yourself, we're on the way! You're one step closer to changing your negative thoughts and ideas of who you are.

Remember—they're only thoughts. We owe it to ourselves to untangle the web of inaccurate ideas that keeps us stuck in age-old patterns of doubt and criticism. The ability to harness and change your power is here and now.

After you have identified the positive and negative messages you're listening to, here are a few suggestions.

First, look at your list again.

Now, take the most salient ones and the most troubling ones from the list.

Say them aloud one more time. Are they true today?

Remember—you're no longer the child listening to an omnipotent adult, peer, parent, or spouse. You can assess the value of these judgments on your own.

How many from the list can you throw away right now?

Which ones are still somewhat accurate?

Which ones do you think you can work to change?

You're an adult with your own life. It's time to hear your own thoughts and beliefs. Listen to who you really are, rather than what someone told you that you were.

Every thought you're thinking or hearing inside shapes your future. Thoughts can propel you forward—or hold you back.

Which thoughts would you prefer to listen to? The ones that move you forward, or the ones that are keeping you stuck?

What we're saying is that it's time to accept yourself. It's time to begin to develop compassion and positive affirmations about you. It's time to forgive and let go. Lack of self-worth means not loving yourself. Can you really afford having low self-worth on the dating scene? It's time to embrace change and the healing process.

Most of us are givers to everyone except one person: yourself. It's time for us to be kind and generous to the person who needs it most!

Building a Fortress of Self-Esteem

Take a deep breath while you're reading this section. Relax your body slowly, head to toe.

Your mind is a tool. You should be in control of your mind, not the other way around.

Forgiveness is key. Now, forgive yourself.

That's what self-love is all about. This is a crucial step in moving forward to finding success in love. Self-acceptance is the key to positive change—and to romance.

Here are some suggestions—and they may seem obvious, but they're easy to forget!

- Be nice to yourself.
- Focus on what you can change; leave what you can't change behind.

- Celebrate and appreciate the small stuff.
- Do what makes you happy.
- Catch your self-criticisms and add a positive affirmation instead.
- Catch your thoughts: Are they true?
- Repeat positive affirmations to yourself often, such as:
- I am beautiful, lovable, happy.
- I am grateful, healthy, eternally young.
- I have wonderful opportunities to choose from.
- I am lucky.
- I love and approve of myself.

Feel free to add your own affirmations based on what you need to believe.

Keep thinking positively! What you choose to think about yourself becomes true for you. If you believe you're lovable and loving, then you will be.

When you find yourself thinking critically or negatively, that will also become your reality. So don't let it!

Repeat this message to yourself over and over (100 times a day, if needed): *I approve of myself.*

For additional steps toward developing your self-esteem, get Louise Hay's book *You Can Heal Your Life* (see more suggestions in the Appendix).

Your Self-Concept in Relation to Finding Love

Here's a way to view your self-concept as it relates to choosing a partner—we find that making these lists really does help!

How do you view yourself? What are your life values?

Get out that pad and pen again. Jot down a new list! Write down what's most important to you.

Write down what's most important in a partner. Place them in order from most important to least. Make sure to include some of the following points:

Children
Family
Money
Religion
Career
Health
Personality
Physical appearance
Humor
Empathy
Social skills

Look at your list again. Choose the top three priorities. What does it tell you about your priorities? Which are needs and which are wants? Is this the "you" that you want guiding your dating world?

These essential needs should be shared with a life partner. They are your priorities and require optimum compatibility for success in attaining happiness. Since these essential needs are most important, they should be nonnegotiable. You must learn to take these top values very seriously.

For example, if you really want kids in your life, know that. Own that. And act on that in your dating life. Don't waste time!

If he doesn't want kids, then that's a major conflict. You're not going to change his mind on such a major issue. Maybe he's not the one for you. So think about moving on, before you get emotionally involved. When you own your priorities, things suddenly become crystal clear—which is good for your peace of mind.

Expanding Your Comfort Zone

As a reminder, keep in mind that if you have a healthy self-concept, healthy self-esteem, and a positive sense of self-worth, you will be more open to expanding your comfort zones. You will be more confident about reaching your goals and dreams. This is why we are delving into these concepts: to broaden your dating options and explore new vistas in life and love.

Since our comfort zone keeps us safe and our world predictable, we feel in control. Life goes on the way it always has. But—and this is a big but—if you're going to stay in your comfort zone, you're going to stagnate. You will continue the way you always have, and your future will be just like your past.

We don't think that's what you want. Is it? You're reading this book because you want something different. Correct?

We often define ourselves and our self-worth in this narrow safe haven. We know that stepping into the unknown can be uncomfortable. After all, it invites fear and it can endanger our self-esteem. Change is never easy. But when you do it in small steps, it becomes less scary and more appealing.

Be gentle with yourself. Change can start with an idea, a thought, an action, a new behavior. We know change can be hard. It disrupts our sense of balance, of knowing, of thinking what the future will be like, and of being in control.

But beyond your comfort zone is a whole unexplored world where you can cultivate new ways of looking at yourself. This will change your outlook on your dates, your relationships, your family, your community, and your life.

SELF-ESTEEM OPENS THE DOOR TO EXPANDING YOUR COMFORT ZONE.

Sound good? We thought so! It's an opportunity to deal with challenges and acquire new skills to learn and move beyond the old and familiar.

Here is the richness of life, a place to expand and grow. To look within yourself and set new goals for life and dating and romance—and happily ever after. It's a place to create new dreams, conquer fears, and find a greater purpose.

Sometimes we have to take a leap of faith to achieve our true desires. Be brave! Because change starts with you.

Summary

- Remember that outdated and negative views of yourself are all based on beliefs, not facts.
- Reevaluating and changing our automatic thinking is hard work, but the payoff is huge.
- Be open to moving beyond what makes you comfortable—this is how you find success in love.
- Remember that now is your time, and you're worth it. Seize the moment!

Conclusion

Yes, Happily Ever After Is Possible

Over the course of our careers as a psychologist and as dating and matchmaking consultants, we have heard thousands of personal stories. Stories of hopes and dreams. Stories of romance. Stories of heartbreak.

Just as we help our clients find true and lasting happiness, in this book we have delved into the human psyche and the science behind love, intimacy, and relationships to help you. We have discovered which strategies work—and which ones don't. After all, humans have been pursuing happily ever after for thousands of years, so there's a lot to examine. And a lot to learn.

We understand the highs and lows of romance. We've witnessed the giddiness in finding love the second time around, and we've been there to see the heartbreak of a lost relationship. In the course of almost 40 years in this field, we've seen it all! The messy breakup, a painful divorce, or the death of a spouse. Through all of these crises, we have committed ourselves to gently cradling our clients and to leading them into a safe, secure, optimistic new beginning.

Our practice is based on science, but we bring compassion and intuition to the mix as well. That's how we have matched thousands of singles and guided them along the path to happily ever after. As we prepare to leave you, our reader, as you embark upon your dating adventures, allow us to share a few final thoughts and stories to encourage you even more.

Hope and Patience

The key word in this process is hope. We add a second crucial mindset: patience. Through the inevitable ups and downs of dating, it's important to keep in mind that hope and patience will be your best companions.

It's not easy. We know. Many clients come to us with a host of feelings: disappointment, confusion, resistance, fear. That's a lot to carry.

We help them work through their negative feelings so that they can connect with their inner strength and optimism before they gingerly reenter the dating arena. We encourage them to have faith and trust in themselves.

We also lead them to confront any thoughts or behavioral

patterns that are unknowingly self-sabotaging their chances to a happily ever after. "Whether you're doing anything consciously or not that's ruining your chances at love," we tell them, "it's time to look at those behaviors, understand where they come from, and then resolve them once and for all."

Thanks to our approach, which combines both science and emotion, as well as gentle prodding and nurturance, we have proudly achieved thousands of success stories.

More Success Stories

Take our client Debbie, a friendly and energetic lady tragically widowed in her late 40s. She was pessimistic about ever finding love again. After losing the love of her life and being overwhelmed by anguish for a decade, she began to venture into dating again.

As we guided Debbie to develop self-awareness and confidence, she was eventually available for a new and courageous journey into the world of love. We were able to show her that every love is different. We assured her that the feeling that no one could or would ever replace her beloved was normal—and that it was also normal to seek love in her life again.

So Debbie persevered in dating. We coached her throughout, reminding her that hope and patience would see her through. She's now happily married and living in Palm Beach.

Dan was typical of many of our clients. He's a highly successful CEO and a leader in his industry. Dan is highly selective and most discerning—both in the boardroom and on the dating scene. While he strives for excellence in every aspect of his life, making smart choices in his emotional life didn't come naturally. Through our consulting sessions we challenged Dan to open himself up to new opportunities and to make smarter choices in dating. Our goal was to help Dan find the love he deserved, and more importantly, to help him discover who he was, what he wanted, and what was most important to his happiness and success. Through sessions of guided soul-searching, we helped Dan break through. He was able to identify his values and goals and better understand how to recognize sustainable chemistry. Dan did the hard work of shedding old behavior patterns. It led to his meeting Leticia, now the love of his life. They are happily married.

Finally, there was Carly. Like so many of our clients, she was reeling from a broken marriage born of betrayal. She was confused, angry, heartbroken, and terribly wounded. While she had been dating online for a few years, she confessed to us that this technology wasn't serving her well. The bells and whistles of this dating process, as well as the sheer number of choices, left her disappointed and confused.

We provided Carly with our effective multidisciplinary counseling combined with our handcrafted process—offering personal guidance, the science of attraction, and matchmaking. We knew that the dating apps weren't designed to examine, search, and deliver her personal objectives. By exploring and healing Carly's past relationship challenges and her physical, emotional, and intellectual needs and goals, we were able to match her with relationship-ready men who met her needs. Soon enough Carly had a new strategy and fresh insights to help her navigate the complicated and risk-filled dating scene. She was able to make smarter choices. Because of her openness and willingness to step outside her comfort zone, Carly is now engaged to a wonderful, like-minded man. We can't wait to attend their wedding next autumn in Chicago.

The Current Dating Scene

We have some good news for you from the front lines: there are more singles today than ever. In 2017, the US Census Bureau reported 110.6 million unmarried people over the age of 18. That's 45.2% of the American adult population. And ladies, this is truly exciting! That means there's a huge array of choices for you. And dating app technology has evolved, making it much easier to find a life partner.

We understand that some people are reluctant to jump back in, even with those great odds. You may have been told that the odds of a middle-aged woman finding love are the same as them winning the lottery. If you believe this nonsense, it will become your truth. Don't let it! There are millions of eligible men out there. You're one in a million.

You may have had an unsuccessful relationship or lost a loved one. You're afraid of rejection. But there's no need to give up or feel desperate.

Being defensive, angry, and bitter only backfires. What's the formula for success on the dating scene? Being patient, having faith, and looking within. To be successful in love doesn't involve a major mystery: our happiest clients learned to expand their comfort zone, identified self-sabotaging tactics, stopped putting materialistic desires above values, and searched for inner truths.

As we tell our clients, there's every reason to be optimistic about finding a suitable partner. It's a matter of soul-searching and making any necessary adjustments, accepting the challenge of dating, deciding how you wish to meet someone, and beginning anew.

While it is scary at first, we hope you will find a way to see it as fun and exciting. Once you let go of the past and openly, optimistically approach the future potential of finding love again, you will enjoy the dating adventure.

Let this book be a road map to lasting happiness. Benefit from the years of experience we bring to the table. Read this book and reread it until you're comfortable dating and moving forward.

Humans have been falling in love for tens of thousands of years. This is not a mystery that can only be solved by a privileged few. The key to finding the perfect partner is based on science and the right kind of chemistry. And that's not merely sexual chemistry. In this book we've explained the difference.

So here's hoping we have been a valuable resource for you, and that we've helped you on your way to achieving your goals and dreams! We would really like to hear your success story.

Please share your experience by emailing us at: nancy@matchmakersguide.com or visiting us at matchmakersguide.com. Keep the faith. You're much closer than you think!

Resources

Here are some of our favorite resources related to topics discussed in this book, should you wish to delve deeper.

Books

Gary Chapman, *The Five Love Languages*, Chicago: Northfield Publishing, 2015.

Erika Ettin, *Love at First Site*, Austin, TX: River Grove Books, 2014.

Helen Fisher, *Why We Love*, New York: Henry Holt and Co., 2005.

John Gray, *Men Are from Mars, Women Are from Venus*, New York: HarperCollins, 1992.

Lori Gottlieb, *Marry Him*, New York: New American Library, 2010.

Rachel Greenwald, *Have Him at Hello*, New York: Random House, 2010.

Louise Hay, *You Can Heal Your Life*, Carlsbad, CA: Hay House Inc., 1999.

Harville Hendrix, *Getting the Love You Want*, New York: Harper Perennial, 1988.

Esther Hicks and Jerry Hicks, *Ask and It Is Given*, Carlsbad, CA: Hay House Inc., 2004.

Evan Marc Katz, *Why He Disappeared*, https://www.evanmarckatz.com/products/why-he-disappeared, 2010.

Judy Kuriansky, *How to Love a Nice Guy*, New York: Doubleday, 1990.

Amir Levine and Rachel Heller, *Attached*, New York: Penguin, 2011.

Terri Orbuch, *Finding Love Again*, Naperville, IL: Sourcebooks Casablanca, 2012.

Online Citations

Brené Brown podcast *Unlocking Us*

Brooke Castillo YouTube

Amy Cuddy TED Talks

Elegant Introductions, www.elegantintroductions.com

www.evanmarckatz.com

Hay House podcast *You Can Heal Your Life*

Oprah podcast Super Soul Conversations

Esther Perel YouTube

Tony Robbins Workshops

Teachings By Abraham YouTube

About the Authors

Nancy Gold Zimmer and **Barbara Black Goldfarb** have been best friends for 35 years and are the unstoppable team behind Elegant Introductions—an award-winning leader in the dating industry that provides a personalized luxury matchmaking service to singles. Driven by their mission to bring more love into the world, Nancy and Barbara have provided dating and relationship advice on major news outlets such as ABC, CBS, and NBC as well as in numerous national publications. In order to reach a broader audience with their mission and message, they have written the book that you now hold.

Nancy Zimmer holds a PhD in psychology from the University of Miami and completed additional training at Harvard University. With 35 years of experience as a relationship coach and matchmaker, Nancy brings with her a unique perspective on what makes relationships flourish and what makes them wither. Nancy has personally counseled thousands of clients on their relationships and has mastered the field of relationship psychology—from the universal desires we all hold to the unique challenges faced by only a few. She is a world-renowned expert on dating and mating and is sought out by clients looking for her advice on how to get from an initial introduction to their happily ever after.

Barbara Goldfarb holds bachelor's and master's degrees from Johns Hopkins University and a master's degree from the London School of Economics. She serves as the chairperson of several nonprofit boards of directors and sits on the boards of several other organizations. With her worldwide network of philanthropy, she has made thousands of romantic introductions and identified the secrets to identifying which ones will spark and which ones will fizzle. Creating countless introductions, Barbara advises singles on what sparks chemistry from the first glance, coaching them on the style, etiquette, and conversations that will make a lasting impression. Using her experiences and the thousands of hours of post-date feedback that she has collected, Barbara's fine-tuned approach has successfully coached and matched hundreds of singles in finding love.